Atlantic
Crisis

By Robert Kleiman

Atlantic Crisis

American Diplomacy

Confronts

a Resurgent Europe

SIDGWICK & JACKSON
London   1965

First published in this edition by
Sidgwick & Jackson Limited 1965

COPYRIGHT © 1964 BY ROBERT KLEIMAN

Printed in Great Britain by
Fletcher & Son Ltd, Norwich

To Jane

Contents

Author's Note

THE ASSASSINATION OF John F. Kennedy may make some of the judgments in this book, most of which was written before his death, seem somewhat harsh. But the decision not to soften them is one which, I feel sure, he would have approved—both as a writer and maker of history.

No setback in office, except perhaps the Bay of Pigs, was more disturbing to the late President than de Gaulle's veto of the American design for the Atlantic future. In the period that followed, the Kennedy administration devised a new strategy to seek the same ends by other means. But the President himself remained puzzled about what had gone wrong, and he sought through official and private inquiries to clarify it. All through his last months in the White House, the questions this book attempts to answer continued to loom large in his thoughts.

I am grateful to Eric Swenson of W. W. Norton for a brief delay in publication which has permitted me to include, mainly in the last chapter, some of the views and early policies of President Johnson on the issues treated here.

January 15, 1964

Preface

THIS SLENDER VOLUME, prepared originally as a private background paper for the Council on Foreign Relations, is an attempt to unravel a mystery. Few diplomatic bombshells since the war have produced as much surprise, shock, dismay, and universal puzzlement—or have caused as much havoc—as de Gaulle's January 1963 press conference. For months afterward—and to this day—participants in the events recounted here and observers near and far have asked themselves and each other, "What happened? What went wrong with Kennedy's 'Grand Design'?"

Prior to launching a new three-year program of Atlantic policy studies, the Council felt it would be useful to seek answers to these questions from several observers who had followed European and Atlantic affairs closely in recent years: a Frenchman, a Briton, and two Americans, one resident in the United States and the other in Europe. The last was myself, and this book is the result.

The origin of the phrase "Kennedy's Grand Design" has been lost to man. It was a misnomer when it entered common use. Some in Europe, including General de Gaulle, read into it objectives that were foreign to its aims. Others, at times, wondered whether there was any grand design at all.

Dean Acheson was asked about it in May 1962 and, according to *The Times* of London, he replied: It "comes from the Press Club bar. Walt Rostow [State Department director of policy planning] has inherited a project of trying to write down everything that has gone on and trying to tie it together. I believe the psychiatrists call this rationalization."

Acheson's quip contained some truth. The core of the "Grand Design" was the idea of an Atlantic Partnership. It began to come into focus for some Administration officials in the fall of 1961. But it was many months later before President Kennedy embraced the concept. And, until January 1963, the Grand Design remained a direction rather than a policy, a perspective toward the future rather than a concrete program to be implemented. The setback it suffered, in this writer's view, stemmed as much from this flaw as from the machinations of Charles de Gaulle.

The Grand Design grew out of Britain's decision, in the summer of 1961, to seek entry into the Common Market. This decision dramatized for Washington the beginnings of a united Europe, which promised to place a new Giant on the world stage.

Within the Common Market, the European nations were eliminating tariffs among themselves. To reduce discrimination against American goods, they offered to negotiate substantial across-the-board tariff cuts with the United States. The President had inadequate authority to take up this offer under the expiring Reciprocal Trade Agreements Act. A radical new bill was drafted, with authority to reduce most tariffs up to 50 percent and some to zero. And the Trade Expansion Act was made the centerpiece of the Kennedy legislative program for 1962.

To some of the President's advisers, the prospect of an unprecedented trade deal between the United States and a united Europe opened vistas of a far broader nature. America's commitments abroad had led to a chronic payments imbalance and a dangerous outflow of gold and dollars. The dollar outflow hampered efforts to stimulate the lagging growth rate of the American economy. It was becoming evident that the United States could not much longer carry worldwide defense and aid burdens alone. But little additional help was to be expected from the European allies individually. Britain's entry into a united Europe, it was thought, would bring into being a partner capable of sharing the load.

President Kennedy gave public support to the idea in his July 4, 1962 speech in Philadelphia:

Acting on our own, by ourselves, we cannot establish justice throughout the world; we cannot ensure its domestic tranquility, or provide for its common defense, or promote its general welfare, or secure the blessings of liberty to ourselves and our posterity. But joined with other free men, we can do all this and more. We can assist the developing nations to throw off the yoke of poverty. We can balance our worldwide trade and payments at the highest possible level of growth. We can mount a deterrent powerful enough to deter any aggression. . . .

I will say here and now, on this day of Independence, that the United States will be ready for a declaration of interdependence, that we will be prepared to discuss with a united Europe the ways and means of forming a concrete Atlantic partnership.

Why did de Gaulle try to thwart this concept of the Atlantic future? Why did he veto Britain's entry into the Common Market? Was this setback unavoidable? What errors did the U.S., Britain, and other Europeans commit? Is de Gaulle's "Non" really irreversible? Where does President Johnson stand on these issues? Can Atlantic Partnership still be achieved? These are some of the questions this book tries to answer.

The reader should be warned that much in this book is written from a Paris-Brussels viewpoint and that many of its thoughts are more generally held in the six Common Market nations of continental Europe than anywhere else. This was done for two reasons: it is a viewpoint that Americans need to understand more fully; and it is a view I share.

During fifteen years as a correspondent in Europe, with many trips to the United States, I have been impressed repeatedly by something that might be called "the influence of geography on history." The world looks different when regarded from Moscow, or Bonn, or Paris, or London, or Washington. It not only looks different, but it *is* different—just as the speed of an object, as the theory of relativity teaches, varies with the speed of the observers who are viewing it.

Nevertheless, the viewpoint in this book is not that of a continental European, nor of a Frenchman, pro- or anti-Gaullist, but that of an American who cannot help examining the world with American eyes. The events here recounted in which the United States participated could not have been described without the generous help of many American officials, high and low, in Europe and in Washington. For the European sections, I have relied primarily on scores of interviews with the diplomats, military men, officials, and cabinet ministers in Paris, Brussels, London, and Bonn who either participated in the negotiations personally, or prepared the briefs for them, or read the minutes of the conversations upon which both the narrative and the analysis in this book depend.

Accounts of what took place at a diplomatic conference, even when honestly told (which is not always the case, either at the time or later), can vary as much as those of an automobile collision. Historians undoubtedly will see these events in better perspective when all the documents have been released, when the actors have published their own accounts, and when some of the threads, followed here over a four-year period, have unwound a bit further into the future. The immediacy of events can be a handicap as well as a benefit, but the journalist does have one vital advantage: he can talk to the participants at first-hand while the details are fresh in their minds and he can question them privately both before and after their meetings and decisions. The contrast between remarks made "before" and "after" provides some of the most useful grist for his mill—particularly when the accounts of the ministers can be checked with the medium-level officials who do the real work and are often less interested in protecting political reputations. It is this kind of detective work that provides the fascination of a reporter's life—and out of it, many of the happenings described in this book have been reconstructed.

It is to these medium-level officials—who would be better served by anonymity—that I owe the deepest debt, and to those ministers and ambassadors who deal in fact rather than fancy.

Among my recent colleagues of the press corps in Europe, I owe special gratitude to David Schoenbrun, Joseph Fromm, Robert Doty, Crosby Noyes, Curtis Prendergast, B. J. Cutler, Frank White, Arnaud de Borchgrave, and Don Cook.

Among those who were kind enough to read the original background paper and provide invaluable comments for its revision, I am most grateful to Hamilton Fish Armstrong, Miriam Camps, William Diebold, Jr., Hedley Donovan, Theodore Geiger, Carroll Kilpatrick, Robert Lubar, Richard Mayne, Jean Monnet, Edward P. Morgan, Jacques van Helmont, Theodore H. White, and those who, holding official posts, must remain unnamed.

I am deeply indebted to the editors of *U.S. News & World Report,* who enabled me to study and report on the political, economic, and military affairs of Europe and the Atlantic Alliance for fourteen absorbing years, and particularly to David Lawrence, Owen L. Scott, Howard W. Flieger, and John R. Fleming.

The starting point for this study was a series of editorial essays written at the suggestion of John B. Oakes, whose later generosity provided the essential time needed to revise the original manuscript.

As Bureau Chief of CBS News in Paris in 1962-63, I benefited from the assignments of Burton Benjamin, Isaac Kleinerman, and Robert Skedgell in acquiring useful background that later helped in writing this book.

The love and forbearance of Jane Eakin, my wife, whose artistry I can never hope to equal, made this a book-birth without agony, if not without pain.

Without the initiative and encouragement of Harold van Buren Cleveland, of the Council on Foreign Relations, this book would neither have been undertaken, written, nor published; and my warmest thanks go to those who brought this collaboration about: Porter McKeever, Ben T. Moore, and Marshall D. Shulman.

Needless to say, what follows was written as a report *to,* not *by* the Council on Foreign Relations. And while this distinguished body deserves whatever credit may derive from this study, which it stimulated, all the errors of fact, analysis, and judgment which it may contain are my own and can not be attributed either to the Council, the good and wise people listed above or the many unnamed who helped to inform me.

ROBERT KLEIMAN

January 6, 1964

*Atlantic
Crisis*

Chapter 1

The Veto

AT 3 P.M. on January 14, 1963, white-gloved hands parted the brocaded curtains in the Salle des Fêtes of the Elysée Palace. A tail-coated huissier announced, "Monsieur le Président de la République!" The familiar towering figure in a gray double-breasted suit strode through the opening, mounted a small podium and sat down behind a table covered with red velvet fringed with gold. Alongside the platform, in order of rank, sat the Premier and all twenty-one Cabinet Ministers of the French Government. High overhead, eight enormous crystal chandeliers lighted the scene.

It was the ritual opening of a semi-annual Charles de Gaulle "press conference," with eight hundred journalists in attendance. A dozen questions were invited at the start, then grouped by subject, summarized by de Gaulle, and answered in a series of eloquent fifteen-minute speeches. With no follow-up questions to divert attention, the histrionic performance built from climax to climax. Only an initiate could have guessed that most of the questions had been planted ahead of time; that every reply had been written out in longhand during the previous week, then pains-takingly corrected; that every phrase had been memorized in advance.

When the eighty-minute meeting was over, it was clear that Britain would be excluded from Europe's six-nation Common Market. The U.S. offer of Polaris missiles had been rejected. The dream of an Atlantic partnership seemed smashed.

All this, carefully planned for public consumption, oc-curred without the courtesy of prior private notice to any of the eight Governments directly involved, not even the Government of France. There had been strong indications of what was coming, but no clear official warning.

On the contrary, only ten days before, one of America's most skillful diplomats, Ambassador Charles Bohlen, had discussed the Nassau Polaris offer with de Gaulle. He left the Elysée Palace with the definite impression that de Gaulle's unenthusiastic reaction was a prelude to prolonged negotiations. At no point in the forty-five-minute tête-à-tête did he hear de Gaulle say, "I am not interested by any-thing you propose"—a phrase that, informed sources say, later turned up in de Gaulle's own minutes of the conver-sation.

Three days before the press conference, on Friday Janu-ary 11th, Britain's Edward Heath had called at the Quai d'Orsay. There had been press reports on Wednesday that de Gaulle now felt Britain would act as America's "Trojan Horse" if admitted to the Common Market. Heath asked whether there were any political conditions for Britain's entry into this economic community. French Foreign Minister Maurice Couve de Murville replied: "If agreement can be reached in the technical negotiations at Brussels, no power on earth can keep you out." Yet, a fortnight later in Brussels, on instructions from de Gaulle, Couve de Murville halted the negotiations in their sixteenth month with a firm French veto. "L'Angleterre," he said, "n'a pas la possibilité d'entrer." Entry is not open to Britain.

How did this all come about? Why did it happen in just this way? Why wasn't British entry just talked to death by technical obstruction, as could so easily have been done? The last two questions have a bearing on the first.

De Gaulle's fondness for high drama in the affairs of state is well known. The great leader, he has written, must wrap himself in mystery and cloak himself in silence so that his occasional declaration will explode as a clap of thunder upon the political scene. This had something to do with the manner of the break. So did the literary quotation with which de Gaulle opened an early book, *Le Fil de l'Epée:* "To be great is to sustain a great quarrel."

But, above all, Charles de Gaulle held his press conference because he wanted history to know that he, and he alone, had shattered the "Grand Design" he believed John F. Kennedy was pursuing.

Britain was the victim of the operation, but one day might be reprieved to join the Continental Six. The more important target was the United States. A French cabinet minister put it this way a year earlier: "De Gaulle wants to end the American hegemony in Europe." Just as Lenin, by intention, split all the socialist parties of the world at one blow, simply by creating the Comintern, so did de Gaulle envisage history's account of his press conference—as the single master stroke that separated the Atlantic world into two entities, the American-led "Anglo-Saxons" and the French-led Continental Europeans.

Nothing has pleased de Gaulle more since January 1963 than, on one hand, to be attacked as the sole villain of the piece and, on the other hand, to be complimented as the leader of a "revolt of Europe" against U.S. domination. This is the role in which he wants the world to see him.

But it would be an error for others to believe that drama is reality, however well a press conference is staged. No European "revolt" either preceded or accompanied the French President's January coup. Nor was de Gaulle solely responsible for this setback to Western unity: he had a lot of help from his adversaries. Over the previous three years, Britain, the United States, the "Europeans" of France, the integrationists of Belgium and Holland, and the "Eurocrats" of Brussels all contributed. Their errors, confusions, and divisions helped create the circumstances that both led to de Gaulle's maneuver and enabled it to succeed. Though there was no single villain in the piece, a single vice often appeared, the most international of vices—nationalism.

To GRASP what happened and to gauge the possibilities ahead, one must be clear about de Gaulle's objectives, his personality, and his method. The manner in which the French President broke off the Brussels negotiations was more suited to relations between enemies than friends. Understandably, as a result, there has been a tendency in Washington, London, and elsewhere to say, "Nothing can be done with de Gaulle." One U.S. diplomat phrases it this way: "He's not negotiable." This writer does not agree.

The General is certainly a hard man with whom to negotiate. He is dedicated to the greater glory of France and little concerned about the interests of others. He assumes that statesmen of other nations are equally guided by self-interest and that alliances do not eliminate national rivalry. That is why he often vents irony, his only humor, against the United States, a nation he considers a necessary military ally, but nothing more. He is convinced that any nation capable of hegemony will seek to exercise it; thus, the United States, by the nature of its power position, is bound to be hostile to what he feels to be the legitimate national ambitions of France.

De Gaulle himself in the mid-1950's best described the sentiments about France that are his central guide. "All my life," he wrote in his memoirs, "I have thought of France in a certain way . . . as chosen for an exalted and exceptional destiny. Instinctively I have the feeling that Providence has created her either for complete successes or for exemplary misfortunes. If, in spite of this, mediocrity shows in her acts and deeds, it strikes me as an absurd anomaly, to be imputed to the faults of Frenchmen, not to the genius of the land. . . . France is not really herself unless she is in the front rank. . . . only vast enterprises are capable of counterbalancing the ferments of disintegration inherent in her people. . . . In short, to my mind, France cannot be France without great-ness."

In his efforts to enhance the "grandeur" of France, the General can draw upon a panoply of talents; he is blessed with remarkable intellect, an unusual memory, a broad grasp of history, and a literary style as masterful in French as is Churchill's in English. He prides himself on his realism and he can be courtly in manner. Yet de Gaulle's words and actions sometimes are such that even friendly statesmen privately accuse him of megalomania. Some of the paradox lies in the way he thinks about himself, less as a man than as a historical personage; he often speaks and writes of himself in the third person. It is not given to many men to save their country twice—once, in 1940, from the disgrace of military defeat and again, in 1958, from the danger of civil war. But there is more to it than that. The General's desire for "vast enterprises" is not new. Three decades ago, he wrote that great leaders are "remembered less for the usefulness of what they have achieved than for the sweep of their en-deavors." And he added that, in leadership, "the question of virtue does not arise. . . . Every man of action has a strong dose of egotism, pride, hardness and ruse." All this, com-bined with the determination to have his own way, makes de Gaulle an extraordinarily difficult ally.

Yet the inflexibility of which de Gaulle is accused is not always the result of personal stubbornness; he employs it as a calculated tactic. Churchill, during the war, once bela-bored him for his intransigence and urged him to yield to Roosevelt from time to time. De Gaulle replied: "You can, because you are seated on a solid State, an assembled nation, a united Empire, large armies. But I! Where are my resources? . . . I am too poor to be able to bow." De Gaulle spent the war years negotiating from weakness and became a master of the art. When he returned to power in 1958, he became enmeshed for four years in a war in Algeria which he had expected to wind up in three months. In his conflicts with the United States then, as in World War II, his only means of pressure was to withhold or partially to withdraw cooperation from the Alliance. Or to threaten to employ as a "balancing element over against the Anglo-Saxons" a cautious French rapprochement with the East—as he did in his approaches to Russia in 1942-45 and in his moves early in 1964 to open diplomatic relations with Peking.

De Gaulle recognizes the importance of America's nuclear umbrella, without which, as he said recently, "the fate of the world would be rapidly settled." But he feels that his bargaining leverage lies in the fact that France, "despite the present inferiority of her (military) means . . . is politically, geographically, morally, militarily essential to the coalition." The methods that served the General so well in weakness are now too well-tested to be abandoned in strength. Denial of cooperation and inflexibility continue to serve de Gaulle as tactics. But inflexibility is not rigidity. The General knows how to bend when necessity imposes or when flexibility pays.

In his day-to-day decisions, the French President is an empiricist; he is critical of doctrine and dogma. Ideology, he said recently, "is only a cover for ambitions . . . it has been that way since the world was born." The great leader needs only a few principles to guide him. Action, de Gaulle has written, must always be "dictated by circumstances."

Whether dealing with friend or foe, the General prefers political warfare to diplomacy, and he practices a curious mixture of the two. He can create a superb illusion of decisiveness and finality, as he did in January 1963. But he knows that nothing is final in this world except the grave. Some of his most decisive stands have been followed by concessions, as in the March 1963 coal mine strike and in the step-by-step disengagement from French Africa.

A few years ago, in a conflict with Parliament over veterans' benefits, de Gaulle announced imperiously that "le Pouvoir ne recul pas"—the public powers do not retreat. Within a few days, one observer commented, "They don't retreat, but they're certainly dancing around." Within weeks, de Gaulle's Prime Minister retreated for him on several fronts.

De Gaulle hates to admit the validity of ideas he has not originated himself. He likes to launch his concepts in vague new phrases for that reason, as well as to conceal, until he can judge from the reactions they arouse, the exact content he wishes to give them. He dislikes negotiating on the proposals of others. He will at times concede more than is necessary by making a new proposal that enables him to call the final agreed plan his own. In the Algerian peace negotiations, Minister for Algeria Louis Joxe assured the General that a compromise could be reached on Algerian demands for sovereignty over the oil-rich Sahara. But the French

President refused and broke off the talks. A few weeks later, in a new proposal, de Gaulle himself offered Algeria the Sahara—without the benefits, for France, of compromise.

All during the spring of 1963, de Gaulle rejected German demands for regular meetings of Britain with the Six and the Common Market Commission to discuss mutual economic problems. Early in July, he went to Bonn with his key Ministers to frame common policies under the new Franco-German Treaty. The meeting made little progress. The Germans made it clear they would not move on agricultural problems of interest to France until the issue of "British contacts" had been settled. A few days later in Paris, through his Foreign Minister, de Gaulle made a "new" proposal—virtually the same arrangements for Britain the Germans had urged, and somewhat more than they had expected to obtain.

De Gaulle is not only a great statesman, but a great politician, much as he hates the word. His tactics are sometimes brilliant, often potent, usually unique—but, almost always, pragmatic. He tries to employ what he once described as the key to Napoleon's successes: "He excelled in adapting his ideas to circumstances which he never failed to study with concentrated attention. . . . There is not the faintest hint in any of his plans or orders of generalized theory."

Long silences and cryptic comments are among de Gaulle's oldest devices. "There can be no prestige without mystery," he wrote in 1932, "for familiarity breeds contempt." In 1963, one of his Ministers commented: "It's like listening to the Oracle at Delphi; when we leave a Cabinet meeting there are always five interpretations of his remarks."

Mystery sometimes is a cloak for indecision; *Hamlet* is one of de Gaulle's favorite plays. Though he believes that leadership is "the constant taking of risks," those who have worked closely with him have often found him cautious, sometimes too much so for their tastes. They say that he rarely makes a major move without evaluating the forces in play with intricate care. He spends much of his time alone thinking; apart from his military aide, only three members of his staff have regular access to him. Before acting, he likes to test the atmosphere with trial balloons; at times he employs elaborate feints and intricate stratagems. He rarely forgets for very long that "politics is the art of the possible" —even when, with extraordinary persistence, he pursues objectives that could only become possible many years later.

De Gaulle's successful exclusion of Britain from the Common Market was not plotted long in advance, as some believe. It came, as we shall see, at the end of an extraordinary concatenation of circumstances, many fortuitous. It was a near thing. It might never have happened if some of the links in the chain had been forged differently by others.

In a California speech in March 1963, Dean Acheson said of de Gaulle: "He can and does in time recognize the inevitable and adjust his conduct to it, as he did in Algeria. It has been wisely said that 'the mode by which the inevitable comes to pass is effort.' The power of the United States to shape the inevitable for General de Gaulle is immense."

If this is true now, it certainly has been so in the past. Yet, in the years preceding January 1963, the United States and Britain neither "shaped the inevitable" for de Gaulle, nor negotiated seriously on his fundamental demands; nor did they seek to do both at the same time. Any of these courses of action, followed with unity, consistency, and foresight, would have constituted a policy that could have succeeded. But a policy to unite the West was precisely what was lacking at that time, despite verbal commitment to distant goals, such as an "Atlantic Community."

Chapter 2

De Gaulle and Kennedy

CHARLES DE GAULLE has been described as "a man of the day-before-yesterday and of the day-after-tomorrow." He lives in the past and in the future. Much has been said, with justice, of his nineteenth-century views, of his archaic nationalism. But something must be understood of his "futurism," and that of other Europeans, if we are to see why the policies of London and Washington ended in Britain's exclusion from the Common Market and de Gaulle's rejection of the Nassau Polaris offer.

Again and again in de Gaulle's eloquent speeches and memoirs, he talks of "the current of history" which must guide nations and leaders in their great decisions. De Gaulle's genius has been his ability at crucial moments to sense and ride with history's tide. In 1933 he foresaw the role of mechanized armor in World War II. Before most of his compatriots, he sensed the coming doom of the Hitler era in 1940 and the collapse of the colonial era in the years preceding his return to power in 1958. He was the first statesman of note to predict the current Sino-Soviet conflict. "De Gaulle's decisions are often wrong," one of his Cabinet Ministers said recently, "his predictions—never."

The historic tide that de Gaulle senses now is a shift in the balance of power within the Western world. The American dominance that marked the 'forties and 'fifties is challenged in the 'sixties. A new power is foreshadowed in the West, a strong, united Europe, increasingly independent of the United States financially, economically, and, perhaps ultimately, in other fields.

The "little" Common Market, as now constituted, is not as small as it seems with Britain freshly subtracted from it. Its population is 170,000,000. Its economy is about as powerful as Russia's, its living standards much higher. Its growth rate over the past decade has been twice that of the United States. Its gold and foreign currency reserves have soared to a level significantly higher than those of the United States; in 1952, even after the Marshall Plan, they were less than one-sixth as large.

The backing of Europe's central banks and treasuries today stiffens the dollar somewhat as U.S. aid supported Europe's currencies during the Marshall Plan years. There has been a dramatic reversal of roles. During the 1961-63 period, the United States had to ask continental Europe first for a $3 billion line of credit and then for another $1.9 billion in treasury bond purchases and swap arrangements.

In the financial and economic fields, therefore, the balance of power within the West already has shifted significantly. Another decade of growth combined with real progress toward political unity could make the six-nation Common Market, without Britain, an entity more nearly approaching the dimensions of the United States and the Soviet Union, whether or not it matches them in all fields.

Roughly equal status with the U.S. and Russia in world affairs has long been de Gaulle's chief ambition for the European power he sees ahead. He seeks to advance French "grandeur" by uniting Europe. He realizes that a nation of forty-seven million with a national income one-ninth that of the United States can only be a second-class power if it stands alone. But, unwilling to merge the French identity in the kind of federal union most non-Gaullist Continentals want, he has proposed a loose "Union of States" leading toward confederation. He was prepared for a time to accept British participation and he knows that ultimately it may be unavoidable both for defense purposes and to counterbalance a Germany more powerful than France. But he prefers the present six-nation configuration because it is, as has been said, "small enough for France to lead and big enough to lead Europe."

De Gaulle's bid for leadership often has been resisted in Europe; his tactics have been deplored; his methods have been attacked as ruthless, Machiavellian and destructive of the community spirit on which, alone, unity can thrive. But it must be recognized that the objective he seeks—equal status for Europe in a world of continental giants—evokes a powerful response both in the Common Market and Britain. De Gaulle was by no means the first to see this even if, when he did, he moved purposefully to encourage and exploit Europe's desires. Equal status is the aim that leads many Europeans, including the "Father" of the new Europe, Jean Monnet, to urge an integrated European nuclear deterrent. They see it as a way to escape the proliferation of national forces—small, inefficient, expensive and dangerous—without remaining forever dependent on the United States for their entire nuclear defense.

"A [U.S.-European] relationship of two separate but equally powerful entities." This is not a phrase used by de Gaulle to advocate a "separatist" Europe. It is the concept of his chief organized opposition in the six nations of the Common Market. It is the phrase used by Monnet's Action Committee for a United States of Europe to describe its ultimate objective, an Atlantic "partnership," a word de Gaulle never employs.

This deep European desire for equality with America has been evident in Britain as well as on the Continent. It is a major reason why Harold Macmillan wanted to be inside Europe, rather than outside looking in. De Gaulle's effort to hasten the unification of Europe, under French leadership, helped provoke Britain's Common Market bid. Macmillan later was to state his thesis, so similar to de Gaulle's, this way: "Are we now to isolate ourselves from Europe, at a time when our own strength is no longer self-sufficient and when the leading European countries are joining together? . . . There remain only two national units which can claim to be world powers in their own right, namely the United States and Soviet Russia. . . . A divided Europe would stand no chance of competing with these great concentrations of power. But in this new European Community . . . a new organization is rapidly developing with the ability to stand on an equal footing with the great power groupings of the world."

After January 14, 1963, the British muted this view and emphasized their American ties in an attempt to isolate de Gaulle. Viscount Hailsham, speaking in New York on January 22, described as "ill-founded" the "fear which is sometimes expressed on the European side of the Atlantic of a community which is dominated by the United States." But the tone was quite different in the original text of his speech, prepared before de Gaulle's January 14 veto and distributed to the press. There the British Cabinet Minister cautioned President Kennedy in these words: "During his election campaign, your President described his future position, if elected . . . as Commander-in-Chief . . . of the forces of the free world. Yet this is precisely what he is not if the allies to which he is bound are not to be deprived of the very independence for which they are prepared to unite. The superiority in numbers, wealth and strength, and therefore in influence and initiative, of the United States is not in question. Nor is its integrity of intention or generosity of character. . . . But have Americans paused to reflect that an alliance in which all the advanced and sophisticated technologies were left to one of the partners, and the rest were relegated to supply a complement of conventional arms in war, and in commerce a modest contribution of Scotch Whiskey and compact cars . . . would not ultimately succeed in retaining the loyalty of European electors?"

Voices of this kind made little impact in Washington before January 1963. They coincided by historical accident with the advent of a new President who, at that time, was tuned in on a totally different wave length. President Kennedy campaigned and assumed office to re-assert American, rather than joint U.S.-European leadership of the free world. His vigor in carrying out that pledge contributed to a rapid deterioration in U.S. relations with two key allies, Germany and France.

What de Gaulle did, through intransigence, to bring this about is only too well-known. But it is useful to examine some of the things the United States did, or failed to do, in the practice of Alliance politics during the first two years of the Kennedy administration.

IN JUNE 1961, when Kennedy and de Gaulle met in Paris, the General proclaimed his high regard for the "intelligence and courage" of the "new young American President." He described Kennedy as "a true statesman, who chooses his goal and holds his course." De Gaulle's respect, if not his affection, for Kennedy far exceeded that for his wartime colleague, Dwight D. Eisenhower. Yet Eisenhower maintained a working relationship with de Gaulle that fell apart in the Kennedy era.

More than a year earlier, at the medieval Château de Rambouillet, de Gaulle emerged from a one-hour tête-à-tête with Eisenhower, bid the U.S. President goodbye, then unexpectedly took the U.S. Secretary of State, Christian Herter, by the arm. He led him into a neighboring room, sat him down and proceeded word by word to repeat what he had just said to Eisenhower privately.

"It was clear that de Gaulle just did not believe that Eisenhower understood what he was talking about," a high U.S. diplomat said.

On the contrary, after his meeting with Kennedy in June 1961, de Gaulle felt that he was dealing with an intellectual equal. He told his Cabinet he was overwhelmed by the dimensions and complexity of the U.S. President's worldwide problems, after Kennedy's exposition of them—and by the awesome responsibility Kennedy carried for controlling and, if necessary, employing America's vast nuclear power. He paid Kennedy the highest compliment he could pay anyone. He said to one visitor, "C'est un homme responsable." He meant that Kennedy was a man who could speak for America, a man who would exercise responsibly the enormous responsibility that he bore.

Why did the two men not meet again?

In June 1961, de Gaulle proposed that they meet twice a year, and the two Presidents decided to get together once more before the year was out. They agreed, in the interim, to have a tripartite military study made of the strategic, nuclear and defense problems that had divided France from the U.S. and Britain for three years. De Gaulle in September 1958 had addressed a memorandum to the U.S. President and the British Prime Minister proposing that France be made an equal partner in what he considered to be U.S.-British direction of the West's global strategy. The fundamental proposal in this memorandum, in de Gaulle's view, had never really been answered, despite evasive replies from London and Washington and numerous meetings related to the subject. It remains in substance, he feels, unanswered to this day.

Nine weeks after the two Presidents met, Kennedy sent Secretary of State Dean Rusk to Paris to propose a new Western initiative in the Cold War. He wanted the West to invite Russia to a Four-Power Foreign Ministers' conference on Berlin.

There was a crisis atmosphere in Germany. Khrushchev had announced that "all time limits have expired" on his Berlin demands. Fear of a new blockade had stimulated a vast exodus from East Germany through Berlin. Rusk, supported by British Foreign Secretary Lord Home, argued that an invitation to an East-West conference would delay for a time Khrushchev's threat to sign a peace treaty and turn over Berlin's access routes to East Germany. French Foreign Minister Maurice Couve de Murville objected. Khrushchev, he said, would take the move as a sign of Western weakness; de Gaulle would never agree to negotiate under Soviet duress. An increasingly angry argument over tactics went on for three days, revealing sharp differences in approach.

"Khrushchev does not want war," said Lord Home. "Negotiation will lead to a Berlin settlement."

Said Couve de Murville: "Negotiations can only lead to major Western concessions to maintain, at best, the physical status quo in Berlin. Why should we be in a hurry to start them?"

Rusk argued: "Negotiations are unlikely to lead to a

Berlin settlement. More likely, they will fail. We may be heading toward a first-class crisis that can lead to war. Public opinion will not understand why this has come about unless we demonstrate, through negotiations, that we have done everything in our power to avoid war."

Replied Couve de Murville: "Public opinion is not important. We are dealing with the national interests of the Great Powers. What is important is the effect on Khrushchev."

Said Rusk: "Public opinion may not be important to France. But it is vital to the United States and other countries."

Rusk took the issue directly to de Gaulle in a call at the Elysée Palace. He told the French President that Kennedy was determined to talk to the Russians. De Gaulle replied brusquely that the U.S. was free to invite Russia to a conference but that, if it did, France would not participate.

Rusk later described de Gaulle's tone in this meeting as "peremptory." Relations between the two men were such that, prior to Rusk's next visit, the American Ambassador and the French Foreign Minister felt it necessary to urge de Gaulle to be polite to the American Secretary of State. Thereafter, he was. It did not make him more cooperative.

De Gaulle's tactics in this dispute had been foreshadowed by his behavior previously in the United Nations and NATO. But the Berlin clash with Kennedy elevated into a doctrine the French policy that later spread to other fields, such as East-West disarmament talks—the doctrine of "nonparticipation."

Erection of the Berlin wall, on August 13, 1961, muted the conflict for a few months. But President Kennedy returned to his Berlin conference proposal in the fall. The issue was argued bitterly until December, when the NATO Ministerial Council, for the first time in its twelve-year history, not only failed to reach agreement but issued a "split" communiqué, fourteen nations more or less for contacts with Russia, France against.

A direct telephone line to de Gaulle, which Eisenhower had installed, got its first and only use during this crisis. With an interpreter in the circuit, Kennedy called and argued his case unsuccessfully for forty-five minutes. The result was predictable, if only because de Gaulle's hatred for telephones is such that he makes fewer calls in a year than Kennedy, as President, made in an average afternoon.

Kennedy remained convinced that there was a danger of war through miscalculation over Berlin. To obtain new Soviet guarantees for Berlin, he was prepared to grant Khrushchev some of the additional recognition the Russian sought for the East German regime. He was ready to join with Khrushchev in other measures to "stabilize" the status quo in Berlin and Germany. Meanwhile, talks would reduce tension. As Churchill had said, "Jaw, jaw is better than war, war."

To de Gaulle, all this meant that Kennedy and Rusk, at best, did not understand the problem of Europe's security. His suspicion was that the U.S. was seeking a worldwide *détente* with Russia at the expense of Germany and Europe. At the very least, he told one visitor, Kennedy seemed prepared "to sacrifice Germany to save Berlin"; but Berlin could not be saved this way; its geographical position would enable Russia to resume pressure any time it wished. The only way to protect Berlin, de Gaulle told Kennedy in June 1961 and subsequently, was to make it clear to Khrushchev that the West would use nuclear weapons if necessary to defend the city. He was convinced that Khrushchev would not risk war.

De Gaulle had no objections to the status quo; he was in no more of a hurry to reunite Germany than Khrushchev. But the status quo meant nonrecognition of East Germany. Additional recognition of the East German regime and measures that would "formalize" the status quo would work to the West's disadvantage. The West Germans would feel that their allies had given up all hope for the ultimate re-unification of Germany. They would come to believe that reunification could be obtained only from the Russians. Sooner or later then, de Gaulle was convinced, the West Germans would turn toward the East.

Somehow, during this dispute, Washington came to believe that the issue it faced was whether or not to negotiate with Russia. The more important problem—how to unite the West for talks with the East—was impatiently pushed aside. The United States unilaterally opened discussions with Moscow, first on Berlin, then on disarmament. De Gaulle sulked in his eighteenth-century Elysée Palace.

The U.S.-Soviet talks solidified the Paris-Bonn Axis. Adenauer was as unenthusiastic as de Gaulle, though less willing to break openly with U.S. policy. White House advisers made it clear from the start that Kennedy, unlike Eisenhower, would not accept "a German veto." After one tense session between the President and Germany's Chancellor at the White House in November 1961, both men ordered the minutes of the meeting burned ("They forgot to cut off the interpreters' tongues," a de Gaulle aide quipped later).

The longer the U.S.-Soviet talks went on, the more they rankled. In May 1962, Adenauer finally exploded publicly. "The conversations have not been crowned with success," he said, "and I don't see why they should be pursued." Adenauer's opposition reinforced de Gaulle's recalcitrance.

In this controversy, the Kennedy-de Gaulle meeting projected for late 1961 was postponed. The tripartite strategic study, for which such high hopes were held, never was undertaken. De Gaulle wrote to Kennedy in August 1961 again urging tripartite political and strategic cooperation with "common organizations to prepare the decisions." And in January 1962 he once more proposed "that the three Great Western Powers . . . institute an organized concert." He suggested a permanent tripartite political commission and military staff that would prepare decisions for the three chiefs of Government in foreign policy and strategy, then follow up their execution. Neither proposal received a Kennedy reply.

Many intermediaries tried to bring the two Presidents together. But de Gaulle refused to go to Bermuda to meet with Kennedy and Macmillan in December 1961 or to Washington to meet with Kennedy alone.

Again and again, Kennedy sent Dean Rusk to Paris to test the atmosphere. André Malraux and other self-appointed French intermediaries came to Washington. The French Ambassador in Washington and the U.S. Ambassador in Paris went far beyond their instructions in repeated efforts to bring their chiefs together. But the two Presidents never met; both argued there was no point in talking when they were so far apart.

In similar circumstances, President Eisenhower made three trips to Paris to see de Gaulle in a single nine-month period. Eisenhower wanted de Gaulle's participation in a Summit Conference with Khrushchev. He did not feel there could be any humiliation in the leader of the world's most powerful nation bowing in protocol to a weaker ally, or even in accepting rebuffs. And he was exasperated during one visit to the point where he referred to de Gaulle's "stubbornness" four times in a single toast.

To win his way, Eisenhower made concession after concession to the French President's prestige. He accepted Paris as the site for the four-power meeting. He postponed the encounter six months. And he yielded to an extraordinary French timetable. This included two Western Summit meetings in Paris, state visits by de Gaulle to England and America, an eleven-day Khrushchev tour of France to match Khrushchev's previous eleven-day tour of the U.S. —and time for France to explode its first two atom bombs, bracketing the Khrushchev visit. In return for this scenario, Eisenhower got what he wanted, de Gaulle's agreement to an East-West Summit.

Kennedy, on the contrary, failed to budge de Gaulle an inch on anything. He found that he could talk with Macmillan—who made a point of seeing the President twice yearly and conversing with him frequently by phone—without compromising the Kennedy concept of American leadership. But he was unwilling to accept the kind of tripartite policy-making with France which alone could have elicited a degree of cooperation from de Gaulle.

The breakdown in relations was epitomized—and completed—by the handling of the Nassau Polaris agreement. Kennedy and Macmillan published their agreement in a communiqué. They sent this public document to de Gaulle with, in effect, a two-sentence covering letter, inviting him to adhere to the "Anglo-Saxon" project. If, instead, the two statesmen had flown from Nassau to Paris to discuss the plan before it was hardened by public release, it is conceivable that they could have succeeded, at the very least, in opening a prolonged negotiation that might have covered Britain's entry into the Common Market. Succeed or fail, the effort would have been worthwhile, once the decision had been taken to offer the Polaris both to Britain and France.

Even so, the Nassau communiqué initially elicited an ambivalent reply from de Gaulle. In this reply, in public remarks, and in a private talk with U.S. Ambassador Bohlen on January 4, 1963, de Gaulle clearly indicated his conditions for a negotiation on the Polaris offer.

De Gaulle said, in effect, that the offer had no interest for France as long as it did not include what the U.S. already had assisted Britain to obtain—the know-how for building nuclear submarines and warheads for the missile. Ambassador Bohlen, stretching the letter of his instructions though not the spirit—he had been told not to let the conversations break down—replied vaguely that the proposals should be considered "as the beginning, not the end" of a negotiation. But de Gaulle had sent his own Ambassador, Hervé Alphand, to ask President Kennedy whether the Polaris offer included technical assistance with submarines and warheads. Kennedy's reply, Alphand had reported, was noncommittal.

Having received the Nassau proposal in the form of a published communiqué, de Gaulle answered in kind. He turned it down in a public press conference. Neither before nor after the January 14 press conference did he incorporate his reply in a private message to Macmillan or Kennedy.

Chapter 3

Nassau

AFTER JANUARY 14, the French spread the myth that it was the Nassau agreement that led de Gaulle to exclude Britain from the Common Market. Foreign Minister Couve de Murville reportedly gave this explanation privately in Brussels on January 16 at a dinner of Common Market Ministers. He said Britain at Nassau had put her nuclear forces under American command, and he implied that this had made Britain an American satellite. Later, Prime Minister Georges Pompidou publicly said that at Nassau "Britain has shown that she is tied first of all to the United States, which is not in Europe." He said Britain could have chosen instead to link her nuclear forces more closely "with European forces, notably the French." Gaullist parliamentary leaders have made much of the fact that Britain negotiated for sixteen months with the Common Market, but reached a major defense agreement with the United States in forty-eight hours at Nassau.

De Gaulle himself was careful not to link the two issues

in his formal press conference. But in informal remarks at a reception for National Assembly deputies, he said: "England has turned over to the Americans what meager atomic forces she had. She could have turned them over to Europe. Well, she has made her choice." After a later reception, deputies said de Gaulle had charged bad faith on Macmillan's part. They quoted him as having said: "At Rambouillet, Mr. Macmillan came to me to say that we ought to unite our two forces. Several days later he went to the Bahamas. Naturally, that changed the tone of my press conference."

The facts are somewhat different. The nuclear issue was always in the background in Britain's attempt to enter the new Europe. At the end, it played a critical role. But it didn't happen in the manner the French now suggest.

The Nassau agreement, in fact, was opened to France precisely to avoid a conflict with de Gaulle that, it was feared, might impede or even destroy Britain's Common Market bid. It was a move that undoubtedly would have stayed the French veto at Brussels if the U.S. had succeeded, as almost happened, in opening a negotiation with de Gaulle on the Polaris offer.

It was not Nassau that decided de Gaulle against British entry into the Common Market. Weeks before, as we shall see, many factors had led him to the conclusion that he should and could end the Brussels negotiations. Six days before the Nassau communiqué, the French President already had indicated his decision to Macmillan in their chilly meeting at the Chateau de Rambouillet; he said there virtually all he later repeated at his January 14 press conference; and he proposed British "association" with the Common Market, implying that London should withdraw its application for full membership.

At Rambouillet, it was not Macmillan who mentioned Franco-British nuclear cooperation. It was de Gaulle, and he did it in a most cautious manner. Interestingly enough, the French President, who dislikes the role of supplicant, neglected to include this remark in his minutes of the meeting. The question came up neither in the conversations about the Common Market nor during Macmillan's comments on the Skybolt controversy and the impending Nassau conference. It came up very briefly during discussion of the Concorde project for an Anglo-French supersonic commercial jetliner. De Gaulle, according to the British minutes, hinted that similar cooperation might usefully be undertaken in missiles. Macmillan was noncommittal. His attempts earlier to draw de Gaulle into a discussion of the nuclear problem in the framework of NATO reorganization had been cut off short.

"It isn't worthwhile discussing NATO," de Gaulle said, "because France will be in it less and less."

During discussion of the Common Market negotiations, Macmillan repeated his previous assurances on British readiness for political union, including a common defense policy. This had always been understood to imply joint research, development and production of arms in the future. At the same time, Macmillan confirmed press reports of a possible Polaris deal with the U.S. He told de Gaulle he was determined at Nassau to obtain "an effective alternative" if the U.S. abandoned development of the Skybolt air-ground missile. The Prime Minister made no attempt to explain, nor did de Gaulle ask, how these two policies could be made compatible.

Skybolt, a bomber-launched ballistic missile with 1,000-mile range, would have extended until 1970 the life of the obsolescent British V-bombers, which soon may be unable safely to penetrate Russia's increasingly effective air defenses. When he obtained Eisenhower's pledge in 1960 that Britain could buy Skybolt, once developed, Macmillan based the future of Britain's nuclear deterrent on it and abandoned development of the British medium-range ballistic missile, Blue Streak. Neither France nor Britain had a second-generation deterrent in sight, although the French were hoping to develop a solid-fuel MRBM by 1970 to replace the Mirage IV bomber. The door was open for Franco-British or broader European development of a medium-range missile for the 'seventies. It was clear that this door would be closed if London, by purchasing Polaris missiles, committed the British deterrent to an American-made delivery system until perhaps 1980.

How could Britain expect to enter an economic, political, and military union with Europe in 1963-64 and leave its nuclear deterrent outside until 1980? Macmillan may have had in mind an answer to this dilemma: an American Polaris offer to France as well as Britain. But he did not discuss it with de Gaulle at Rambouillet. He did mention it at Nassau; but the offer to France was primarily an American initiative. The Prime Minister did not attempt to influence either its substance or its form to make the offer more palatable to de Gaulle. On the contrary, Macmillan's single-minded pursuit of a new nuclear-weapons system for Britain —that he could announce immediately and defend as independent—led him at Nassau to discourage American proposals for a more effective approach to France.

Macmillan met Kennedy in Nassau on December 18, 1962, two days after he had left de Gaulle. He had intended to press for Skybolt, not for Polaris. But shortly before Kennedy arrived, Macmillan learned from an American correspondent that the President, in Washington, had told television interviewers that Skybolt development for U.S. forces definitely would be abandoned. When the President's plane landed, out stepped David Ormsby-Gore, Britain's Ambassador in Washington and Kennedy's old friend. He told the Prime Minister that aboard the plane he and the President had arrived at a new proposal. The U.S., which had been paying all the bills, would continue trying to develop Skybolt, for British use only, if Britain would pay half of the remaining development cost.

The new price was too high for the Prime Minister. When he sat down with the President and Kennedy formally offered the fifty-fifty deal on Skybolt, Macmillan commented: "I'm afraid the lady's reputation has been damaged beyond repair."

As the discussions turned to Polaris, de Gaulle's shadow lay across the table. Even before leaving Washington, Kennedy had been advised by Ambassador Bohlen and others that it would be disastrous to give Polaris to the British and not offer it to the French. Macmillan's comments on Rambouillet reinforced this feeling, although they did not indicate that a French veto at Brussels was imminent.

The Nassau offer to de Gaulle seemed to involve a revision of U.S. nuclear policy toward France. It proposed to sell major elements of a nuclear delivery system that would be nationally owned and operated by France though assigned to a NATO command. It accepted a substantial advance toward tripartitism in NATO—a special status for France, as well as for the U.S. and Britain, in the projected NATO nuclear force. Other NATO countries were invited to participate only in multilaterally owned, mixed-manned vessels, which could not be unscrambled for national use. France, Britain, and the United States would participate with national units that could be withdrawn on national decision when "supreme national interests are at stake."

Why, having gone this far, did President Kennedy withhold from France the submarine and warhead technology available to Britain?

The answer lies, in part, in the nature of Nassau. Washington and London were equally responsible for the predicament in which Kennedy and Macmillan found themselves. The Pentagon had precipitated the ill-advised Skybolt controversy with a computer decision to cancel development of the missile; the difficult project was held to be proceeding too slowly, too expensively and too uncertainly and, in any case, it had been rendered unnecessary by the success of the Polaris and Minutemen missiles. The political consequences for Britain and for U.S. relations with London and Paris were overlooked or underestimated. The U.S. Embassy in London warned that the Conservative Government could fall on this issue; it urged that Macmillan be given a maximum of time in secrecy to make new plans and to prepare public opinion, if Skybolt cancellation could not be avoided. But the President nevertheless accepted and later re-confirmed Secretary McNamara's timetable: a budget ruling abandoning Skybolt for U.S. forces before the end of the year. It was a decision that should have been postponed until new arrangements could have been made with the British that would not have endangered vital U.S. objectives abroad; the bill for a six- or twelve month postponement would have been cheap compared with the political losses that later ensued. But there was a general budget-trimming exercise underway that was permitted to take precedence over foreign policy goals: the White House was determined not to exceed the peak budget deficit of the Eisenhower era.

When McNamara telephoned the bad news to British Defense Minister Thorneycroft early in November 1962, the Briton said he would have to study alternatives. His tone encouraged McNamara to believe the British reaction would not be explosive. The U.S. Defense Secretary expected a request for Polaris and planned a London visit. The visit was thrice postponed; but London, meanwhile, made no counterproposals. The Royal Air Force opposed a shift to Polaris, which would transfer to the Navy its strategic nuclear role; it hoped the U.S. Air Force would win its fight to save the Skybolt program. The Royal Navy, curiously enough, was almost equally reluctant to take on Polaris; it preferred to devote its limited funds and technicians to new aircraft carriers. None of this was realized in Washington. When McNamara came to London on December 11, he was surprised to hear Thorneycroft argue at length the case for Skybolt in an attempt to preserve the existing arrangements.

When the conversation finally turned to Polaris, according to British officials, McNamara said that the United States would be prepared to sell the submarine-launched missiles to Britain, but that Britain's Polaris force would have to be committed "irrevocably" to NATO. Thorneycroft replied angrily that this would never be accepted. If the United States wished to substitute Polaris for Skybolt, the terms should be the same; any commitment to NATO command would have to be a British decision.

Meanwhile, the U.S. Air Force had leaked the Skybolt controversy to the press. In hopes of forcing Washington to reverse itself, Britain's Conservative Party had joined in whipping up a public clamor over "the American betrayal."

By the time Macmillan came to Nassau, he was caught in a political crisis that was partly of his own making. Labor Party leaders and Conservative backbenchers opposed to Common Market entry already were attacking him for "scuttling" the Commonwealth and, as Hugh Gaitskell put it, for preparing "the end of Britain as an independent nation." Macmillan insisted he had to leave Nassau with an independent deterrent or be accused of surrendering the last vestiges of Britain's national interests.

Kennedy was prepared for the argument that the Conservative Government would fall on the issue, and that a Labor Government would oppose Common Market entry. But this was not the argument the Prime Minister made. Instead, Macmillan indicated that the Tory Party, to survive, would be forced to exploit the "perfidious America" issue. The implication was that Macmillan either would be replaced by an anti-American Conservative or would himself take the head of an anti-American campaign in Britain dwarfing the one that followed Suez. This kind of a break with London was something Kennedy had not contemplated and was not prepared to face on the issue of an "irrevocable" commitment of Britain's deterrent to NATO.

As Secretary Rusk, who was not at Nassau, later put it to a visitor who had criticized the "surrender" to Britain at Nassau: "We can't break with Britain. We have to be able to discuss world problems with someone. We can't discuss them with de Gaulle. . . . We and the British don't always agree. But we discuss."

Under these pressures, with the aid of inadequate staffs, the President and the Prime Minister set about resolving in forty-eight hours a complex of problems that had baffled the United States and the Atlantic Alliance for more than four years. The potpourri included America's most complex weapons system and such issues as nuclear diffusion, atomic sharing in NATO, nuclear arming of Germany, and de Gaulle's atomic ambitions. Weeks after Kennedy returned to Washington, scores of experts from the State and Defense Departments, the White House and the National Security

Council were still trying to figure out what the Nassau agreement meant. Macmillan, back in London, stressed his right to withdraw Britain's Polaris submarines from NATO for national use and insisted he had retained an independent deterrent. Administration spokesmen, in Washington, emphasized the multilateral aspects of the agreement and described Britain's withdrawal rights as virtually useless. As for the offer to France, when de Gaulle turned it down three weeks later, its implications were still under study by an interdepartmental task force in Washington that had not yet reported.

In these circumstances, what was the true meaning of the offer to France?

The Kennedy Administration had made a thoroughgoing reappraisal of nuclear policy toward France only the previous Spring. The U.S. Joint Chiefs of Staff had argued that nuclear assistance would win de Gaulle back to cooperation with NATO. Among other things, it would reduce the cost of the Force de Frappe and enable France to make a larger contribution to NATO's conventional forces. This view was supported by General Maxwell Taylor, then the White House military adviser, after a tour of Europe. A similar view was taken by Secretary of the Treasury Douglas Dillon, by Central Intelligence Agency Director John McCone, and by two U.S. Ambassadors in Paris, General James Gavin (France) and Thomas Finletter (NATO).

Secretary Rusk disagreed. He argued that de Gaulle's conflicts with the U.S. and NATO, which were essentially political, could not be resolved that way. He warned that proliferation of nuclear weapons would be stimulated and that Germany would become the next claimant, provoking a dangerous Russian reaction. This view was supported by the President's security adviser, McGeorge Bundy, by his chief disarmament advisers, by the Congressional Joint Atomic Energy Committee, and by NATO's Supreme Commander in Europe, General Lauris Norstad, who had been urging for a long time that the U.S. make NATO, not France, the world's fourth nuclear power.

After weeks of debate, President Kennedy in April 1962 decided to reaffirm existing policy. In a talk I had with him a few days earlier, it was clear that he had already made up his mind. He said he had been unable to get a satisfactory answer from any of his advisers to one key question: "Why would de Gaulle be more cooperative with NATO after he gets his own nuclear force?"

There were other reasons as well. Even before assuming the burdens of office, Kennedy was impressed with the awesome risks of the nuclear arms race. He was determined, while hastening the American buildup, to pursue an arms control agreement with Russia, with a nuclear test-ban as the first step. No objective of his Administration, in the opinion of White House aides, had greater importance in the President's mind. One of Kennedy's first moves in office was to tighten up control of American atomic stockpiles in Europe to reduce the danger of accidental use. In three forums, the U.N., the Geneva disarmament talks, and in negotiations over Berlin and Germany, the Administration sought agreement with Russia on nondiffusion of nuclear arms to "countries not now possessing them." Theoretically, such an agreement would not have affected France, as a country already possessing nuclear arms, or NATO (an alliance, not a "country"). But, psychologically, the President's general concern about proliferation made him reluctant prior to Nassau to consider nuclear assistance either to France or to a NATO force.

The President shared the view, expressed by Secretary McNamara in June 1962, that "limited nuclear capabilities, operating independently, are dangerous, expensive, prone to obsolescence and lacking in credibility as a deterrent"; and that "the creation of a single additional national nuclear force encourages the proliferation of nuclear power with all its attendant dangers."

An equally critical factor, in the President's view, was the need for unified command and control arrangements for the West's nuclear weapons. As McNamara expressed it at Ann Arbor in June 1962, a "strategy of controlled response" required "concentration of executive authority and central direction" of all nuclear forces. The Cuban showdown in October 1962 reinforced this view.

A U.S. monopoly of the West's nuclear weapons obviously would provide the maximum in "central direction." In both the Eisenhower and Kennedy Administrations there was a hope that Britain and France, certainly after de Gaulle, ultimately would contract out of the expensive nuclear arms race. Failing that, integration under NATO command seemed the next best thing.

At Nassau, when Britain in return for Polaris agreed to

commit its deterrent to NATO, it became possible for the
first time to offer France equal treatment without accepting
the concept of a completely independent French nuclear
force. Some members of the U.S. delegation at Nassau had
favored atomic aid to France the previous Spring. Others
thought the time had come to test de Gaulle's intentions.
The General's response would demonstrate whether he was
willing to resume cooperation with NATO and, especially,
to integrate his Force de Frappe under "central direction"
in a NATO command.

One important American participant was so pleased
with this development that he commented: "Thank God for
Skybolt. It has opened the way to getting the French back
into NATO."

President Kennedy was less sanguine. One informed
U.S. official gave this description of the White House view:
"Nobody thought de Gaulle would accept the Nassau offer."

Another high official, who saw the President before and
after Nassau, went further. "Kennedy," he said, "didn't
want de Gaulle to accept the Polaris offer."

What did the President want? He had been urged to
avoid a clash with de Gaulle that would further complicate
U.S.-French relations and Britain's Common Market negotiations. But he remained reluctant to contribute to an independent nuclear deterrent in France or in Europe. His
attempt temporarily to escape this dilemma was described
as follows by a U.S. diplomat:

"The President's objective showed clearly in his instructions to [Ambassador] Bohlen. They can be summarized in

one sentence—'Engage de Gaulle in a prolonged negotiation.' "

The Americans, at Nassau, realized that Britain's Common Market bid was in trouble, although they did not know how close de Gaulle was to breaking off the Brussels negotiations. Macmillan either had failed to grasp or had refused to admit the full significance of Rambouillet. He described the Rambouillet atmosphere to Kennedy. But he indicated that the negotiations would go on and that the outcome would turn on the agricultural issue. Asked whether the Nassau agreement might not affect the Brussels talks, Macmillan replied: "It has nothing to do with them."

The Americans, nevertheless, had heard enough to be seriously concerned about the French reaction to Nassau. They proposed that a discussion be opened with de Gaulle before the U.S.-British Polaris agreement was finalized. But Macmillan insisted that the deal had to be announced before he returned to London. Kennedy finally agreed—and de Gaulle, thus, was presented with a *fait accompli*.

Despite all this, a negotiation with the French President almost was engaged. The Nassau offer tempted the General. His senior Minister of State, André Malraux, arrived at the White House from Paris and told Kennedy that de Gaulle expected a long technical negotiation followed by a meeting of the two Presidents. Yet, a few days later, de Gaulle took the opposite decision. De Gaulle's thought-processes had proved as unfathomable, even for Malraux, as the Mona Lisa smile the Minister had brought to Washington.

The French President had realized, as did Kennedy, that

he could not open a nuclear negotiation with the United States and simultaneously shut the Brussels door on Britain. He preferred to sacrifice an uncertain gain for his "Force de Frappe" rather than stay his hand on Britain at that strategic moment. Furthermore, the seeming ease with which Britain had obtained privileged treatment at Nassau provided a perfect pretext for a dramatic break with the "Anglo-Saxons." Had it not been for Nassau, de Gaulle's closest advisers are convinced, there would not have been a sudden veto. Instead, there would have been a rapid stiffening of the French position at Brussels—something that would have given the British at least one more chance to come to terms. Nassau undoubtedly "changed the tone" of de Gaulle's press conference. Kennedy's opportunity to change its content had been missed.

Essentially, the opportunity was missed because the American President at Nassau and immediately afterward was not prepared to make the choice toward which the Skybolt controversy and the endangered Brussels negotiations had propelled him. He could not bring himself to terminate the special U.S.-British relationship nor to extend it completely either to France or to the new Europe. If Polaris had been offered, not to Britain, but to an integrated European nuclear force based on a joint Anglo-French effort open to others; if the U.S. had offered to transform the Anglo-American special relationship into a U.S.-European special relationship, Atlantic unity might have moved forward rather than backward in January 1963.

Chapter 4

De Gaulle and Britain

In GROPING for a policy toward Europe now, London is handicapped by the "devil theory of history." Most British officials are convinced that de Gaulle, to assure an "inward-looking" Europe, was determined from the start to block Britain's entry into the Common Market. They suspect that de Gaulle's ultimate objective is a deal with Russia. Thus, London now seems to believe that little can be done, except to pursue British national interests, as long as de Gaulle remains in power.

It is useful in this context to look back over de Gaulle's attitude during the three years that preceded January 1963. A good starting point, for irony, is April 5, 1960.

That evening, at Buckingham Palace, where he was temporarily residing, the French President received Her Majesty's Prime Minister for an hour's conversation. It was the first day of de Gaulle's triumphant state visit to England. The ears of both men still rang with the cries of "Vive de Gaulle," shouted unexpectedly by thousands of staid Londoners who lined the streets to welcome de Gaulle's return to his wartime haven. Early in the talk, according to Foreign Office officials in London, the following exchange took place:

DE GAULLE: Is it true, as reported after your Washington visit, that you are contemplating an alliance with Russia?

MACMILLAN: I can't imagine how anything so ridiculous could have been published. I simply warned of the dangers of a trade war between the Common Market Six and the seven nations on the periphery which have united in EFTA [the European Free Trade Association].

DE GAULLE: Why don't you join the Common Market?

MACMILLAN: That would be unthinkable.

What was "unthinkable" in April 1960 became the center of Macmillan's thoughts and actions only four months later. His first soundings were made during a visit with Germany's Chancellor Konrad Adenauer in August. When he next met de Gaulle, at the Château de Rambouillet in January 1961, Macmillan for five months had been cautiously exploring what economic move would permit Britain's political participation in the new Europe.

On the minds of both men was the Summit conference of the Six which was scheduled to meet two weeks later to discuss European political union. De Gaulle repeated several times that this meeting was "not directed against Britain." Macmillan said he too saw a political necessity for a united Europe. And he spoke of the need to make "a good working arrangement of the Six, the United Kingdom and EFTA." The implication was that Britain now was prepared to negotiate directly with the Six and to settle the EFTA problem separately.

De Gaulle replied that he did not envisage limiting the Common Market to the Six. He suggested that British and French experts might examine the possibility of bringing Britain and the Common Market together. . . as British and German experts, whom the French earlier had been asked to join, already were doing.

When the British and French experts met at the end of February, it was announced that they had discussed two possibilities: British "association" with the Common Market and full membership. British talks with the French, Germans, and Italians, and a March-April tour of Europe by the Lord Privy Seal, Edward Heath, convinced London that no satisfactory agreement short of full membership was possible. Moreover, the Six were firm that full membership alone would permit Britain to take part in the political union of Europe—and that, since August 1960, had been Macmillan's primary objective.

In March 1961, U.S. Undersecretary of State George Ball, touring Europe, called to see Heath in London. He was surprised to find the Lord Privy Seal surrounded by all his Foreign Office and Treasury experts.

"What," asked Heath, "would be the American reaction if Britain decided to join the Common Market?"

Ball had no instructions; no policy had been set. The Kennedy administration had been in office little more than two months and it was just about to plunge into the disastrous Bay of Pigs adventure. Some of the President's key advisers were little informed about the Common Market problem. But Ball was not one of them. He was a lawyer who had represented the French Government, the French Manufacturers Association and the European Coal and Steel Community in Washington for many years. He thought fast and replied: "We would consider it a contribution to the unity of the West."

A few weeks later, Prime Minister Macmillan came to Washington. The Common Market was on the agenda, and by this time there was a White House policy that confirmed Ball's earlier reply. Kennedy told Macmillan that the special U.S.-British relationship had no future, that a united Europe would come first in U.S. policy abroad. He said he was concerned about Germany and France. The stability of both hung on aged leaders, Adenauer and de Gaulle. After their departure, France might relapse into instability and Germany would become an unknown factor. Britain's entry into the Common Market could hold the continent steady. As Macmillan described some of the problems entry would pose for Britain, Kennedy said that he would do anything he could to help.

That evening, at a reception, Macmillan three times came up to Ball, took him by the elbow and whispered in his ear: "We're going to do it. We're going to do it."

Much later the French were to claim that Ball and Kennedy pressured Macmillan into his Common Market bid. They said this was a factor in arousing de Gaulle's suspicions that Britain in the E.E.C. would serve as America's "Trojan Horse." But there was no justice to this charge. The Ball-Heath and the Kennedy-Macmillan conversations both took place after the French themselves had publicly urged the

British to come in. In a speech to the Council of Europe on March 2, 1961 Foreign Minister Couve de Murville had said:

Our colleagues in the Six countries and we ourselves have always said that the Common Market was and would remain open for any other European country to join if they wished. We still believe that for some people at least this is a worthwhile prospect and perhaps the only satisfactory solution. *We still hope that there will be a change of mind** in certain quarters whence the response has so far been negative.

· At the end of June, in a speech at Metz, de Gaulle said:

*It is necessary** also that England come into the Common Market, but without posing conditions.

In July 1961, Britain announced its decision, and the formal application was made in August. De Gaulle made his reaction public during a press conference on September 5, 1961:

The six participating nations of the Common Market *have always wished that others, and in particular Great Britain, adhere to the Rome Treaty,** that they assume its obligations and that they receive its benefits. We know very well the complexity of the problem, but it seems that everything is now moving to solve it and, for my part, *I can only be pleased about it,** not only from the point of view of my country, but from the point of view of Europe and, at the same time, from the point of view of the world.

The negotiations opened in Paris on October 10, 1961 and continued in Brussels in November, centering on the

---

* Italics author's.

special arrangements sought by Britain for Commonwealth trade. The Six, from the start, made it clear that Commonwealth preferences would have to be terminated, although transitional and other arrangements could be made to ease the pain.

At the end of November, when he visited Macmillan at Birch Grove, de Gaulle discussed the Commonwealth problem and made it clear that Britain had to make a choice between the Commonwealth and Europe. He repeated that Britain "would be welcome" in the Common Market as "un pays sérieux"—a solid country.

The first difficulties appeared in the spring of 1962. In April, negotiations on de Gaulle's project for political union of the Six were blocked by the Dutch—acting as Britain's agent, the French believed. In May, Britain continued to support the U.S., at a Foreign Ministers' meeting, in the dispute with de Gaulle and Adenauer over Berlin—although London already had quietly withdrawn from the British-Soviet talks that had paralleled the U.S. overture to Russia in 1961. At the same time, at the Athens NATO conference, Britain joined the U.S. in winning NATO agreement to new atomic "guidelines"—over French opposition. During this meeting, the U.S. Secretary of Defense proclaimed a new U.S. strategy for NATO, emphasizing conventional arms. The 1961 Kennedy promise to undertake a U.S.-French study of "global strategy" had not been implemented, and the new "McNamara Doctrine" fed French suspicions that there could no longer be full reliance on U.S. use of nuclear weapons to defend Europe. Meanwhile, the British-Common Market negotiations in Brussels were dragging on endlessly over the Commonwealth issue. Although the French Ambassador in London took a strongly contrary view, Paris began to suspect that opposition within the Conservative party and the Commonwealth would make it impossible for Macmillan to meet the Common Market's entry terms.

A de Gaulle-Macmillan conference had been scheduled for June 2 and 3, 1962 at the Château des Champs, near Paris. A few days before, stories appeared in the British press that de Gaulle was demanding an Anglo-French nuclear deal as the price of British entry into the Common Market. De Gaulle was warned by his Prime Minister and Foreign Minister that this probably was a maneuver to blame him for a British-manipulated breakdown of the Brussels negotiations.

To counter this "maneuver," de Gaulle invited British Ambassador Sir Pierson Dixon in for a talk. It was up to Britain and Britain alone, de Gaulle said, to decide whether it wanted to become part of Europe. He denied that he was "asking" nuclear cooperation as a condition for British entry into the E.E.C.

This curious denial, of course, meant only that de Gaulle would never accept the position of "demandeur," of asking for the aid of others. It did not mean that he did not want British assistance for his Force de Frappe. But it demonstrated how far he was prepared to go at that time to assure that France could not be blamed if the Brussels negotiations broke down.

It was clear that Macmillan understood this when he met de Gaulle at Champs. The Prime Minister spoke with great optimism of his domestic political and Commonwealth problems. Agriculture, he said, only employed four percent of the British population as against twenty percent in France, and he was sure a solution could be found. He said he looked for agreement in principle at Brussels on all major issues during the summer. He was certain he could win approval both at the Commonwealth Prime Ministers' Conference in September and at the Conservative Party Conference in October. After entry into the Common Market, Macmillan said, Britain looked forward to political union with the Six. That would mean close cooperation with France and the Six, not only in foreign policy but also in defense. He spoke for the first time of a European, rather than simply a NATO, defense policy. There was a mention of future Anglo-French cooperation in defense production and research. While no details were discussed or engagements made, de Gaulle emerged with the impression that the door would be open to Anglo-French cooperation in the nuclear defense field after Britain entered the Common Market. There was no indication in the British minutes that cooperation in nuclear arms production, as such, had been discussed. But Macmillan, according to the French minutes, suggested that the two countries coordinate the plans of their nuclear forces for circumstances, should they arise, where the United States might be unwilling to employ its deterrent.

De Gaulle's conviction, after Champs, was that the British "had made their choice—for Europe." He said this to his closest advisers. One of these, his longtime aide and present Ambassador to London, Geoffroy de Courcel, was elated as he rode back to Paris with Sir Pierson Dixon, and he congratulated the British Ambassador. British entry, he felt, was a certainty.

Couve de Murville, in Brussels, told French diplomats his estimate now was four-to-one for British acceptance of the minimum Common Market conditions. The French Foreign Minister retained this view even after final agreement on the Commonwealth issue was blocked in August by a nasty crisis over Commonwealth agriculture and future financing of E.E.C. farm subsidies, of which the French expected to get the lion's share. When the Japanese Foreign Minister, during a visit to Paris in September, asked about the Brussels prospects, Couve de Murville replied, "All the technical problems have been settled." This was not strictly true. But it reflected the French evaluation of where things were headed.

All this is not to say that de Gaulle was overjoyed at the prospect of having Britain in the Common Market. But it is clear that in August, in September, even in October 1962, British entry was still possible.

Certainly, the French never went out of their way to make things easy for London. They were persistent in protecting French economic interests. But at no point was there evidence of a serious French effort to keep Britain out.

The French pressed always for acceleration measures

and completion of as much as possible of the Common Market structure before British entry. They opposed concessions that would weaken economic union. For this reason, they often had the Common Market Commission on their side. When they had the support of the Commission or at least one of the other Common Market countries, the French sometimes fought extended battles before compromises were reached. But they were careful always not to be isolated. When they were, they usually gave ground quickly. And whatever went on when the Six met alone, the French cooperated to assure unity when they met with the British.

The French Government and its negotiators were divided between opponents and proponents of British entry. The top Foreign Ministry official involved was an opponent. He is said to have told de Gaulle six times in two years that the Commonwealth made British entry impossible. "You can have a regional organization or a world organization, but not a regional organization that is worldwide," he said. The top Economics Ministry official involved was a proponent of British entry. He had been an executive assistant to former Foreign Minister Robert Schuman and had collaborated with Jean Monnet in originating the Schuman plan. He refused to go to Brussels for the meetings where the veto was imposed on British entry.

The French Cabinet was divided in the same way. Foreign Minister Couve de Murville was less than enthusiastic about the British coming in. But Michel Debré, Prime Minister until April 1962 and the Cabinet's most fanatical Gaullist, was a strong British advocate. As a Senator, Debré had fought against the Schuman Plan and the European Defense Community. With other Gaullists, he had argued that the "little Europe" of the Six would be dominated by Germany. He believed fiercely that British membership in the Common Market was essential to counterbalance the power that West Germany, with forty-three percent of Common Market industry, might wield in the future. Debré's successor, Premier Georges Pompidou, more or less shared this view.

De Gaulle's own attitude initially, according to his closest advisers, was one of willingness to negotiate joined with skepticism that Britain finally would take the plunge. It was a combination of many factors that led him later to the veto decision. But none of these substantive factors could have been entertained had it not been for a dramatic change in the political situation in France and in the political climate elsewhere in the Common Market in the summer and fall of 1962. Until then, one imperative dominated de Gaulle's thinking: France, under no circumstances, could take the responsibility and the blame for keeping the British out.

There were two stern deterrents to a veto, one external, the other internal. Externally, as long as France's five partners in the E.E.C. strongly favored British entry, there was the danger that a French veto would break up the Common Market. Internally, the very future of the Gaullist regime was at stake. The end of the Algerian war had created the possibility of an anti-de Gaulle majority in the French National Assembly. The Center-Left, which had supported

Algerian independence, and the Center-Right, which had fought de Gaulle's Algerian policy, were united in favor of a supranational Europe, British entry, and NATO integration. A French veto of Britain, opposed by the Five, would have brought down the French Government; a vote of no-confidence by the National Assembly would have been certain. It would have precipitated Parliamentary elections under circumstances highly unfavorable to de Gaulle.

This situation was reversed during the fall of 1962. Internally, the opposition parties were outmaneuvered by de Gaulle. Instead of challenging the Gaullists on European, Atlantic and pocketbook issues, the opposition brought down the Government on terrain de Gaulle had selected: his proposal for popular election of the President. Even so, de Gaulle's majority in the October Constitutional referendum on this issue fell fifteen to thirty percent below previous polls. De Gaulle had threatened to resign unless he received a massive majority. The results were a great disappointment to him. With most of his Ministers, he became deeply pessimistic about the November elections. Prime Minister Pompidou expected the Gaullist U.N.R., already a minority, to lose at least a fifth of its seats in the National Assembly. But de Gaulle's personal prestige and disunity among the opposition parties produced an unprecedented upset. The Gaullists captured thirty-two percent of the popular vote. With the aid of a few Independents, they obtained an absolute majority in the Assembly, the first one-party majority since the French revolution. At home, this meant a free hand for de Gaulle in all fields.

Externally, the French President's freedom of action remained much more limited. He did not want to break up the Common Market to keep Britain out. But by December 1962, enthusiasm for British entry among the Five and in the Brussels Commission had given way to considerable disenchantment. There were mixed emotions over Britain's dilatory negotiating tactics and London's insistence on special arrangements that, many feared, would undermine Europe's economic union. It was this disarray among the Five that made a French veto something that could be entertained as a calculated risk.

"THEY'LL get used to it." This was the cynical comment of a French official as the French veto brought the British-Common Market negotiations to a final halt. A newsman had asked how the Five would react.

The scene was Brussels. The date was January 29, 1963. The Ministers, grim and white-faced, were filing out of the Council chamber. Despite their doubts about the British, the Five were outraged at the unilateral French move. A few minutes before, the Belgian Foreign Minister had called the French veto "monstrous" and had voiced a "solemn protest against the way this decision has been imposed on us." Luxembourg's Foreign Minister had expressed "dismay" and "deep concern." The Italian had warned of "serious dangers." The German had said, "My Government will not give up this project." The Dutch Foreign Minister had said, "It is a black day for Europe."

Yet, within a matter of weeks, it became clear that the Common Market of the Six would go on. No aspect of the January crisis was more significant than the rapidity with which Europe's rage was sublimated, once the initial shock wore off.

Deep suspicion of France certainly will continue as long as de Gaulle remains in power, and Common Market progress will be hampered for some time. But most of the Five were and are less disturbed at the fact of Britain's exclusion than at the ruthless and "unconstitutional" way it was done. That was why the danger of a Common Market breakup—or a refusal of the Five to go any further without a French reversal—evaporated quickly.

Why was this so?

"It's like the prolonged illness of an aged uncle," said one member of the Common Market Commission. "When he dies, everyone is sorry. But they breathe a sigh of relief.

"The negotiations simply lasted far too long. The British should have made a deal in October 1962, after the successful Commonwealth and Conservative Party conferences. Instead, they dug in their heels on a secondary issue and blocked progress for the rest of the year."

Said another member of the Commission: "Everyone felt Britain, like France, wanted a multi-national Europe with itself as the paramount power. If Britain had favored a supranational Europe, she would have had the Governments of the Five and public opinion in France enthusiastically behind her."

Italy's chief negotiator disagreed publicly with Macmillan's statement that the negotiations were halted because they were about to succeed.

"Had this been the reason," said Minister of Industry Emilio Colombo, "there would have been no need for such a violent and immediate break. . . . A large number of problems were still unresolved and France could have easily taken one of those unsettled problems as a pretext for stiffening her attitude and eventually closing the door to further negotiations.

"On the contrary . . . the requirement that economic negotiations . . . stimulate political integration and a common defense [is what led] during the last months of the negotiations to the crisis of mistrust which is at the basis of the failure."

In France, Socialist leader Guy Mollet, long an advocate of British participation, said Britain's attitude had convinced him several months earlier that full membership would be a mistake. He added, "A real association would be worth much more than a false integration."

Maurice Faure, a Radical Party ex-minister and one of the authors of the Common Market Treaty, asked a sympathetic French official to help him draft a major Assembly speech blasting Britain's exclusion. A week later, the speech was still in his pocket. "I went to the provinces for the weekend," he told an aide. "Nobody is disturbed about the British."

A distinguished Frenchman, who has promoted British membership, said: "We must conclude that the French people, who were defeated and occupied in World War II, feel closer to the Germans, who shared the same experience, than to the British, who did not."

In Holland, the rector of the European College, M. H. Brugmans, told the Dutch branch of the European movement: "We must make an end to the situation which, in effect, reduces Europe to the state of a military protectorate of the United States. President de Gaulle has been foresighted in this situation. . . . A political union cannot be supranational at the beginning because no government could give its entire support to such a conception."

In Belgium, Foreign Minister Paul-Henri Spaak encountered violent heckling and stinkbombs at a public meeting where he attacked the Gaullist conception of a European nuclear deterrent, independent of the United States.

The President of the Belgian Senate, Paul Struye, a European integrationist, said: "General de Gaulle is in some ways more 'European' than those who attack him. . . . When he wishes Europe to be as independent of America as possible, politically, militarily and in atomic strength, as well as economically, one can share or not share his views, but it is impossible to deny that his conception of Europe is strongly 'European.'. . . Despite the excessive fear of supranationality, Gaullist policy through the Fouchet Plan has sought a beginning of political union which, to a majority of Belgians, could only have been a first step; but the flat rejection of this plan had no other effect than to block all progress of the European Community toward political union."

In Germany, support for British entry remained stronger than it was anywhere else, except perhaps in Holland. But even here, there was an emotional doubt. One British journalist encountered it in a call on the German Ambassador in London.

"I asked him," said the journalist, " 'What went wrong?' I never got an answer. He spent the whole hour telling me *his* troubles in London, asking me, over and over again, 'Why are we Germans so hated in England, when the French have felt themselves able to become our allies?' "

It was in Germany, too, that the only possible leader of the Five turned out to be the one least perturbed by de Gaulle's January 14 press conference. Germany's aged Chancellor, Konrad Adenauer, came to Paris in the midst of the crisis to kiss de Gaulle on both cheeks and complete a political and military union between the two states. The signing of the new Franco-German treaty of reconciliation on January 23 made it clear that Adenauer was "reconciled" as well to Britain's exclusion from the Common Market. Adenauer ignored pressure from the United States and from powerful forces in Europe which urged him to make his signature contingent on a continuation of the British negotiations.

Adenauer's willingness to abandon the British—and to abandon the American concept of the Atlantic future—was the decisive element that enabled de Gaulle to take his calculated risk and, later, to make his veto stick. The Chancellor, a Rhinelander, had dreamed all his life of a Franco-German entente. He had no liking for the British, and this coolness, in 1961-62, turned increasingly to active distrust of the British attitude toward European union and their efforts, with the Americans, to negotiate a German settlement with Russia over the opposition of Paris and Bonn.

Chapter 5

Britain's Errors

BRITAIN's own responsibility for its defeat was not much less than de Gaulle's. Though it often is forgotten now, Britain's exclusion from Europe for many years was self-imposed and accompanied, later, by proposals that would have thwarted Europe's unification. The suspicions aroused by these earlier attitudes contributed to the collapse of Macmillan's Common Market bid.

London's resistance to European union started the day Europe began to unite, almost fourteen years ago. Before that, in a Zurich speech in 1946, Winston Churchill had proposed "a kind of United States of Europe" for the continent. Clement Attlee had said Europe must "federate or perish." But when the Schuman Plan in May 1950 proposed a limited merger of sovereignty in a limited field, Britain's Labor Government refused to join. It was the beginning of a decade in which the British were to prefer nationalism to any sharing of sovereignty with Europe.

In August 1950, as leader of the opposition, Churchill proposed a European Army. A year later, as Prime Minister, he followed the Labor Government in rejecting both the European Defense Community and the Coal and Steel Community projects. The failure of the E.D.C. could have been avoided had Britain been willing to join, or even to associate itself closely—as Premier Pierre Mendes-France later asked —making the kind of military commitment to the continent that London finally made after the E.D.C. was defeated. The success of the European Defense Community under those circumstances would have made Britain's subsequent entry into Europe far easier. Among other things, the E.D.C. would have led toward a European rather than a French national deterrent, heading off in advance the dispute over French nuclear ambitions that later was to play an important role in Britain's exclusion from the Common Market.

By 1956, Britain's abstention from the new Europe began to be supplemented by proposals that competed with the efforts of the Six and threatened, if successful, to dissolve their embryonic union in wider and looser groupings. Britain sought the kind of international cooperation among sovereign nations that—unlike the moves toward federal union—could never bring about the fundamental change so badly needed by a Balkanized Europe.

On July 11, 1956, the French Assembly in a turning-point debate authorized negotiations for a supranational European Atomic Energy Community in which six countries subsequently pooled sovereignty and resources for non-military uses of the atom. A week later, Britain, which had refused to participate in Euratom, encouraged the Organization for European Economic Cooperation (O.E.E.C.) to push ahead with earlier plans for a seventeen-nation Nuclear Energy Agency without supranational features.

Britain's reaction to the project for a Common Market, from 1956 to 1958, threatened Europe's developing union much more seriously. Britain was invited, but refused to join in drafting the Rome Treaty. For the next two and a half years, London pressed for a seventeen-nation Free Trade Area that would have destroyed the European Economic Community before it began to function. That proposal divided the Six for a long time. When it finally was rejected in November 1958, Britain launched the competing seven-nation European Free Trade Association. It then fought for a preferential tariff deal—the old Free Trade Area in another guise—between the inner Six and the EFTA Seven.

The United States was cool to EFTA from the start, as it had been toward the Free Trade Area plan, once its nature had become clear. In Washington in March 1960, President Eisenhower again told Macmillan that a thirteen-nation preferential zone was as unacceptable as a seventeen-nation zone. It would discriminate against American exports without advancing Europe's economic and political integration. But Macmillan clung to his project. He warned Eisenhower that a "trade war" would divide Europe and NATO. He drew analogies between EFTA and the "peripheral alliance"—including Russia—which Britain had organized to defeat Napoleon. And a few days later, at Buckingham Palace, he told de Gaulle that British entry into the Common Market was "unthinkable."

Four months later, Macmillan had changed his mind. But his reasons for doing so and his subsequent tactics were not such as to expunge, for the Six, the memory of the previous decade. On the contrary, they nurtured the suspicion that one British objective in entering the Common Market was to change its essential character. The accuracy of this suspicion was less important than its existence. Despite differences, none of the Six was fully convinced that Britain, after joining, would work to strengthen, rather than weaken, Europe's unity and independence. None was willing, as a result, to take major risks with the structure of the Common Market to ease Britain's problems.

MACMILLAN moved toward entry into the new Europe in 1960 for the same reason Dyrenfurth and his party climbed Mount Everest: "It was still there." The many in Britain who had been sure the Common Market would fail had been proven wrong. And as Jean Monnet remarked in February 1959:

"The British have a great virtue: they recognize facts. Once the British acknowledge that the Common Market is a fact, they will deal with it."

The fact Macmillan recognized was that the Common Market not only had proved itself a success but that it had done so far more rapidly than anyone had expected. On May 12, 1960, a month after the Macmillan-de Gaulle talk at

Buckingham Palace, the E.E.C. demonstrated its dynamism by the first of a series of dramatic acceleration decisions. The aim of these decisions was to achieve a full customs union in eight years instead of the twelve to fifteen years laid down in the Rome Treaty.

It was not the economics of this that moved Macmillan. True, public support for entry later was sought by claims that the Common Market would revolutionize British industry. But in 1960, only fifteen percent of Britain's trade was with the Six. Exports to the Commonwealth at that time were three times as large. Many of Macmillan's economic advisers and cabinet colleagues were opposed to joining the Common Market. Some never developed much enthusiasm for the idea.

What moved Macmillan most in the success of the Common Market was the historic British fear of a continent organized by someone else. That fear was confirmed at the end of July 1960 when de Gaulle met with Adenauer at the Château de Rambouillet. The French President there unveiled his plan for European political union. He proposed a six-nation Union of States leading toward "an imposing European Confederation"—"the most powerful, prosperous and influential political, economic, cultural and military complex in the world," as he later described it. De Gaulle was moving into the vacuum created when the U-2 incident and the U.S. Presidential campaign removed Eisenhower from the world stage. The French President called for regular Summit conferences of the Six to provide European leadership for the West.

Meanwhile, at the end of May, the East-West Summit conference with Khrushchev had aborted in the wake of the U-2 affair. This was a project Macmillan had originated and to which he had devoted his chief energies for more than a year. It was the basis of his claim to British leadership in Europe—as the honest broker between Moscow and Washington.

Having lost his Summit, Macmillan was "looking for a role." The immediate role Macmillan sought was to place London at the conjuncture of three great circles of influence: Europe, the Commonwealth, and the special U.S.-British relationship. His twenty-year goal, he told one American visitor, was a kind of "Atlantic Union." This plan was plagued by inner contradictions and a failure to establish clear priorities of British interest. It was later to help undermine Britain's approach to the Common Market. But, at the time, it marked a courageous initiative, for it involved, as a first step, British entry into the new Europe.

Macmillan's first stroke on this canvas was recalled recently by a British diplomat: "One day we were buttoning up the final arrangements for EFTA. The next day Macmillan flew to Bonn and we found him, to our amazement, sounding out the old Chancellor cautiously, very cautiously, on a British move into Europe." The date was August 10, 1960.

The caution manifested at the beginning continued to the end—and contributed significantly to Macmillan's undoing. The Foreign Office planning staff had suggested Common Market membership as early as December 1958. By August

1960, twenty months already had been lost in forging the EFTA chain which, later, was to be one of Britain's heaviest burdens at Brussels. Now, in the summer of 1960, Macmillan headed into Europe with what came to be known as his "inching tactics." It was a year later before he applied for Common Market membership, and two and a half years later he was still inching his way along when the guillotine fell.

THE "long, long, so long, so long Brussels conversations," as de Gaulle later described them, opened on October 10, 1961. Seven months and many frustrations later, on May 12, 1962, the Italian Chairman emerged from a Ministerial meeting and announced: "The conference which has just been held between the Six and Britain has been very useful because it has enabled us . . . *to begin the actual negotiations on British accession.*"* He added, on behalf of all Six Common Market nations: "None of the proposals made to the Six by Mr. Heath was considered compatible as a whole with the Rome Treaty or, in particular, with the application of a common external tariff . . . at the end of the transitional period."

Much of the delay during the first seven months stemmed from Britain's attempt to avoid a choice between Europe and the Commonwealth. Heath opened the discussions with a series of proposals that would have maintained a preferential position for Commonwealth exports either in

---

* Italics author's.

Britain or in the enlarged Common Market as a whole. The most critical issue was that of "comparable outlets" for the cereals, meat, butter, and other temperate-zone farm exports of the old white Dominions, Australia, New Zealand, and Canada. Britain insisted on a guarantee that the enlarged Common Market would provide these Commonwealth countries with "outlets for their produce comparable to those they now enjoy."

In all the preliminary talks of the previous year, the Six had made it clear that Britain would have to come within the E.E.C.'s common external tariff. That meant an end to Commonwealth trade preferences. The Six were prepared, at most, to help minimize trade losses for the Commonwealth countries through an assortment of transitional and other measures, some of permanent value, such as liberal trade agreements and reductions in tariffs, a few to zero level. Britain had accepted this in theory, but then had sought substitute arrangements, such as "comparable outlets," that provided preference for Commonwealth exports in another guise. The effect was to block negotiations until Britain yielded in fact, as well as in theory, on the principal of trade preferences. This took many months.

Britain's able negotiator, Edward Heath, was bound by —and often chafed under—restrictions imposed by London in an attempt to carry along a divided Commonwealth, a divided country, a divided party, and a divided Cabinet. Three of the most important members of the Cabinet— R. A. Butler, Reginald Maudling, and Lord Hailsham— were antipathetic to British entry, as were many of the Conservative Party constituency leaders around the country. Macmillan evidently felt that Butler and Hailsham, as his chief rivals for the Party leadership, were potential instigators of a Party rebellion. Their names and Maudling's initially led the field for the Prime Ministership when Macmillan announced his retirement in the Fall of 1963.

Macmillan never succeeded in getting Lord Hailsham to commit himself publicly to Common Market entry. Butler was "neutralized," in a typical Macmillan maneuver, by appointment as head of the interministerial committee that directed the Brussels negotiators. Maudling, as the free-trade area negotiator of 1957-58, was already on record against British entry into the E.E.C. Macmillan first transferred him to the Colonial Office, away from European responsibilities, then rewarded him for his silence in July 1962 with appointment as Chancellor of the Exchequer, though that was the Ministry most directly involved in the Common Market talks.

Meanwhile, Macmillan himself avoided committing his reputation completely to entry into the new Europe. During the ten months that followed Britain's August 1961 application, he maintained the fiction that Britain had not really applied at all! He described the application as a formality to permit negotiations that would enable Britain ultimately to decide whether it wanted to enter the Common Market. This self-evident pretense was harmless at the start. But ultimately it confused and troubled Britain's friends on the Continent, for the Prime Minister until June 1962 refrained studiously from vigorous public advocacy of British entry.

In terms of Conservative Party politics, this was perhaps an exhibition of Macmillan at his most skillful. He avoided an explosion in the Commonwealth and rebellion either in the Cabinet or in the constituencies. He carried his party through a 180-degree reversal in historic British policy without losing a single important Tory leader.

But there is reason to doubt whether this degree of caution was advisable. What Macmillan failed to see was that his biggest problem, as events later demonstrated, was not at home but in Brussels. By making Butler and then Maudling key men in determining the policy and pace of his Brussels negotiators, Macmillan helped assure the long-drawn-out struggle with the Six that later made de Gaulle's veto possible.

The risks of a prolonged negotiation were evident at the time. Many of Britain's friends, including Jean Monnet, urged London to seek rapid agreement on basic principles and the most important problems. The remainder could have been settled at a later, wrap-up stage—or even after entry. Much could have been safely left for the Community's institutions to work out. Rapid entry would have dissipated suspicion of Britain's motives and provided London with powerful bargaining leverage within the Community's decision-making machinery.

"I told the British many times," said a top Eurocrat in Brussels, "that they should consider admission into the

Common Market a victory in itself and not seek an unobtainable and largely unnecessary prior victory on the entry terms."

Heath, however, had other instructions. And he considered it useful, in any event, to educate the Six about the complexities of Commonwealth trade before tackling the critical issues.

During the initial seven months of non-negotiation in Brussels, the British discussed everything from Indian cricket bats to Australian kangaroo meat and Bechuanaland customs procedures.

"Most of us didn't even know where Bechuanaland was," said one of the top negotiators of the Six. "Here we were just beginning to build an economic community in Europe. Suddenly we were confronted with the prospect of absorbing a world-wide trade bloc of 800,000,000 people in 60 countries located on every continent of the earth. The wider the discussions ranged geographically and the more ground we gave on these complicated secondary matters, the less willing were we to compromise on the main problems."

Britain defeated its own purpose, as well, by waging a delaying action on other important issues such as its proposal for zero tariffs on aluminum and twenty-five other raw materials. After the negotiations collapsed, Heath revealed that the British intention had been to seek a "package deal" at the end by bargaining off unrelated points. It was an unfortunate plan, especially since no one understood what the British were up to. These dilatory tactics merely confused and discouraged Britain's friends among the Six, while providing ammunition for those who were unenthu-siastic about British entry.

Throughout, it was the British who determined the pace and substance of the discussions, which centered on their proposals for special arrangements and protocols. When the British sought to negotiate seriously, as they did from May to August 1962, progress was rapid. During this period, there was give-and-take on both sides, and most Common-wealth issues were settled. Agreement even came close on the critical problem of Commonwealth farm exports.

The over-all outlook seemed so good in July that Iain McLeod, the Conservative Party Chairman and Tory leader in the House of Commons, urged that caution be thrown to the winds. He proposed to his Cabinet colleagues that Britain seek a crash negotiation in Brussels to button up an agreement in August before the summer recess. McLeod, according to others present, argued that further delay was dangerous and that the time already had arrived when the Conservative Party could go to the country on the issue and win an early election. If the proposal had carried, Britain would be in the Common Market now. But McLeod was in the minority. The Cabinet consensus was that it was better to await the results of the Commonwealth and Conservative party conferences in September and October.

Both conferences went well. The Commonwealth Prime Ministers, despite many doubts and demands, adjourned without scheduling another meeting prior to British entry. The communiqué said "they recognized that . . . the respon-sibility for the final decision would rest with the British

Government." The Conservative Party conference turned into a carnival. Enthusiasm swept over the delegates, who wore "Yes" badges and voted overwhelmingly for the Government's Common Market policy. Even Rab Butler spoke up for entry, despite his continued resistance to farm concessions in Brussels. He made the main reply to Labor Party leader Hugh Gaitskell, who had charged the week before that Common Market entry would turn Britain into "a province of Europe" and "mark the end of a thousand years of history." Said Butler: "For them, a thousand years of history. For us, the future!"

But when the Brussels negotiations resumed in October, Britain's representatives made no attempt to wind up the Commonwealth issues, which were close to agreement. Instead, to the despair of their friends, they returned to non-negotiation.

United Kingdom agriculture was the issue London chose for this last act of the Brussels drama. It was an issue of particular interest to Butler, who had represented a farm constituency for thirty-five years. The Six, again, were prepared to meet many of Britain's difficulties. Germany's highly protected farmers, almost three times as numerous as Britain's, were the Community's real problem. Over-all, Britain's farmers, relatively efficient, were unlikely to lose income and were almost certain to gain from the local and Community-wide measures everyone knew would be unavoidable to help German agriculture adjust to a single European market. These measures, most of which were still to be worked out, clearly would affect various sectors of British agriculture differently. The Six expected numerous British proposals for special substantive arrangements. Instead, London made an issue, not of farm income as such, but of the administrative system by which it was to be sustained.

The Community's farm system permitted each country initially to keep food prices for its consumers at a level high enough to assure adequate income for its farmers, and it provided that adjustment toward a single price level in the whole Community would come about only gradually. The future Community price level was yet to be determined for various key products, but everyone knew it ultimately would have to be somewhere between the moderate French and high German levels.

Britain's system was one of low food prices for consumers, based on the low world prices Britain paid for its food imports. Domestic farm income was assured by deficiency payments—direct government cash subsidies—to Britain's farmers.

For three crucial months, in the fall of 1962, the Brussels negotiations were blocked by British insistence on twelve, then eight years to make the administrative changeover to the Community's farm system, something each of the Six had done only a few months before. True, Britain's system was completely different from those that had existed previously on the continent, and it required far more adjustment. But this was an issue which Heath had raised in the spring, then abandoned. Its revival took everyone by surprise. None of the Six trusted the British enough to permit them to enter the Common Market without this irreversible commitment to the Community's common agricultural policy. There was fear that London, after entry, would delay its changeover, then exploit differences among the Six and seek to revise the E.E.C. farm policy in the interests of the Commonwealth.

All through the fall, the British refused to budge on the farm system issue. Real negotiations on the Ministerial level never started again after August. Of all Britain's errors, this was the most disastrous.

De Gaulle became convinced that Britain was stalling to await his defeat in the French elections. Other reasons for barring the British accumulated in the fall.

French big business turned against the British in September. Inflation, raising costs, was beginning to price French exports out of the market for the first time in almost four years. The Patronat, the French National Association of Manufacturers, began to argue that French industry would not be able to face British competition on top of the German.

In October, the British Labor Party Conference voted against the Common Market. Later, a series of British by-elections indicated a significant swing toward Labor and a possible Labor victory in the approaching national elections. Labor Party leader Hugh Gaitskell in a Paris visit told Prime Minister Pompidou that his party, which might well form the next British Goverment, preferred "association" with the Common Market to full membership.

Other British Laborites spread the same message elsewhere. Belgian Foreign Minister Spaak walked out of a meeting with a member of Labor's shadow cabinet, Patrick Gordon-Walker, and exploded: "A few more minutes and he would have made me into a Gaullist."

Disenchantment with Britain began to catch hold in most of the Common Market Governments. The Brussels discussions had been underway for fourteen months and only in three of those months had the British really negotiated.

In December, Ambassador de Courcel returned from London to brief de Gaulle before the Rambouillet meeting with Macmillan. Though an advocate of British entry, he had become convinced that Macmillan now hesitated to go to the polls on a Common Market platform. His analysis was that the Brussels negotiations, so far, had settled only half the issues at stake. Macmillan would be unable to make the necessary concessions on the other half in the year preceding an election.

In the strategy sessions in Paris that preceded Macmillan's arrival, there was general agreement that it was intolerable to wait another year for the British to resume serious negotiations. The Germans were holding up implementation of the common farm policy pending British entry. The Dutch were blocking European political union for the same reason. The air had to be cleared. De Gaulle was urged to suggest to Macmillan that temporary, transitional arrangements be sought in the economic field until the British elections. Then, if the Conservatives won, negotiations for

British entry could be resumed. The General listened to all this, but gave no clear indication of what his tactics would be.

Meanwhile, on November 25, de Gaulle had won the heady election victory in France that smashed his domestic opposition. Sometime between November 25 and December 15, the French President took the decision to bar the Brussels road to Britain.

"MANY ripening factors"—as Premier Georges Pompidou later put it—entered into de Gaulle's historic decision. The British Prime Minister was the first to get an indication of de Gaulle's change of heart—and some of the reasons for it —when he met with the French President at Rambouillet on December 15 and 16, 1962, a month before the de Gaulle press conference.

It was at Rambouillet, two years earlier, that the two men had first discussed with such hopeful results the possibility of a British move into Europe. This time, from their first conversation, the British and French leaders clashed.

Later, there were reports that Macmillan had not understood de Gaulle, or vice versa. But the confidential record shows, on the contrary, that each understood the other all too clearly.

Macmillan, in fact, was so shocked by de Gaulle's opening remarks about the Common Market that he insisted that interpreters and his private secretary remain present at all meetings. There were no substantive conversations during walks alone in the gardens as during previous encounters at Rambouillet, Birch Grove and Champs.

De Gaulle's remarks paralleled closely what he was to say publicly a month later, according to French and British officials involved in the talks. The General pointed out that no progress had been made at Brussels since August. He said it had become clear that Britain, as an insular, maritime power would be unable to accept the rules of a Continental Community and had sought to change the Common Market's essential character. He proposed British "association" with the E.E.C., instead of full membership, something Adenauer already had suggested publicly nine months before.

But among de Gaulle's most revealing comments were several that he did not repeat at his press conference.

The French President said that Britain's presence was not helping to unite Europe. On the contrary, it was dividing the Six. He said that Britain's entry would change the "balance" of the Community. It would alter the "weight of France." It would deprive France, within the Community, of the ability "to say 'No' to any country, including Germany."

"Why," asked Macmillan angrily, "why didn't you say this before?"

In part, de Gaulle was referring to Britain's EFTA obligations, which none of the Six was willing to accept. The British in June 1961 rashly committed themselves not to enter the Common Market until all of the Seven had been admitted, in full or associate status. All seven had to "participate from the same date in an integrated European market." This meant prolonged uncertainty as to when Britain could enter, even if agreement were reached. It meant enlarging the Common Market initially to ten or eleven full members. This would have made political cohesion far more difficult to achieve. And it would have required total revision of the Community's voting system. The balance between small and large countries and among the large countries themselves would have undergone a fundamental change.

But even more than the EFTA problem, what de Gaulle was evoking at Rambouillet was the role Britain, at Brussels, had indicated it would play once inside the Common Market. It was a role that not only challenged French leadership of the new Europe, but frequently sought to isolate France within the Community.

Chapter 6

The Critical Issues: Agriculture and Political Union

OF ALL THE factors that led de Gaulle to veto Britain's entry into the Common Market, none was more vital than this: at no point in two years of discussion did Britain, or the United States, seriously seek to come to terms with France on the future of Europe and the Atlantic world.

The British dealt with the six member countries as if all were equal in reality as well as juridically. They behaved as if Dutch support was as valuable as French acquiescence.

"I urged the British repeatedly to deal directly with the strongest critics of their proposals, the French and the Common Market Commission," said a key Eurocrat. "But they preferred to negotiate primarily with the others, playing them off against France. This aroused French suspicions and resentments."

Nowhere was this more evident than in the British approach to the issues of agriculture and political union.

In agriculture, Britain challenged one of the basic economic bargains between France and Germany implicit in the Common Market treaty. It was a deal made at a Heads of Government conference and without it—as Parliamentary debate showed at the time—the French Assembly probably would not have ratified the Rome accords. Under the terms of this bargain, France accepted the competition of German industrial goods, and Germany pledged to open its doors to French farm products—through a single agricultural market with a single price structure in the six countries. Germany and the others could continue to buy foodstuffs outside the Community at lower world prices. But, under a "financial regulation," savings from such purchases were to go to the Community—to be used in substantial part to subsidize French exports and farm modernization.

It took the French four years of tenacious effort and, at the end, a series of all-night meetings to get the Germans to begin to carry out this bargain. A common agricultural policy, including the financial regulation, finally was adopted on January 14, 1962. It was adopted only after the French for fourteen days had exercised their veto to block an advance into the Treaty's Second Stage.

The British raised objections to the financial regulation early in the Brussels negotiations, then dropped the issue. But this re-opened major differences in interpretation among the Six, particularly between France and Germany. On August 4, 1962, the French and Germans patched up some of their differences. But the British went to work in the corridors and got the Germans to reverse their position on the financial regulation a few hours later.

The British move boomeranged. It occurred toward the end of a marathon five-day conference which sought final agreement on Commonwealth issues. On the last two days, the Ministers worked forty-eight hours with four hours' sleep, and the Six, with French agreement, had made many concessions. Only one important paragraph held up agreement on reasonable outlets for Canadian, Australian, and New Zealand foodstuffs in Europe. The financial regulation obviously had to be an integral part of the deal. The Six re-established unity on this issue, with the Germans reversing field again. But the atmosphere by this time had been poisoned. The conference broke down at 7 a.m. Sunday August 5, after a seventeen-hour session, leaving the critical Commonwealth problem unresolved.

The Six suspected that, their terms being difficult, Britain preferred to withhold its final concessions until after the Commonwealth and Conservative Party conferences in the fall. While this disappointed Britain's friends, it was something politicians were prepared to understand. But the tactics Britain had employed during this important August episode aroused suspicion of Britain's intentions.

The question many asked was why Britain did not seek a deal on agriculture with France. The Germans, with high-cost farms, favored a high-price structure for the Community, which would mean high Community output of food. Lower Community prices, which the French and British favored, would restrain output and leave a larger market for Commonwealth foodstuffs. Had the British been willing to wind up Commonwealth preferences and to accept a common market in agriculture, they logically should have sought a Commonwealth solution through a price deal with France. Instead, on this issue as on many others, the British tried to outmaneuver the French by capitalizing on divisions among the Six.

THE obstruction of de Gaulle's plan for political union of the Six did Britain even more harm than the conflict over agriculture. Here, as on so many subjects, the Six were divided badly, and their efforts to reach agreement were continually hobbled by Britain's attitude.

De Gaulle, as we have seen, unveiled his plan for a "Union of States" when Adenauer visited him at Rambouillet at the end of July 1960. He proposed a Summit meeting of the Six in the fall. The Chancellor agreed enthusiastically. But when Adenauer got back to Bonn and took a closer look at the plan with his cabinet, he became convinced he had been taken in by his eloquent French friend. Within a week, he reneged. By emissary and letter, Adenauer told de Gaulle he feared that the project would divert Europe from the road toward federal union, injure NATO, and undermine the existing European Communities. During the next few months, there was a definite chill in relations between the two men. Adenauer, in pique, canceled a long-scheduled Fall trip to France.

A dizzy whirl of diplomatic conferences, nevertheless,

was set in motion by de Gaulle's proposal. De Gaulle put his plan before the Prime Ministers of Holland, Italy, Belgium, and Luxembourg, who came in turn to Paris in September. Meanwhile, Macmillan on August 10 had sounded Adenauer in vague terms on a British move into Europe and had received a warm response. This meeting was followed by high-level British consultations with the Dutch, the Belgians, and the Italians. Italy's Premier Fanfani then met with Adenauer at Lake Como. The debate was embittered when de Gaulle, on September 5, made his plan public in a press conference at which he attacked supranational authorities and proposed a major reorganization of NATO. Finally, in October, French Premier Michel Debré flew to Bonn to appease some of Adenauer's anxieties about de Gaulle's proposals.

By December 1960, when Adenauer finally came to Paris to meet de Gaulle, the outline of a compromise had appeared. It followed more or less the position proposed on November 22 by Jean Monnet in a letter to his influential Action Committee for a United States of Europe.

Monnet saw de Gaulle's plan as an opportunity to make a long first stride toward true political union. He suggested that much of it be accepted but that a number of amendments be proposed, of which two were crucial to keeping open the road toward Federal union. The existing European Communities had to be safeguarded, if not reinforced. And a revision clause in the treaty had to provide for evolution from unanimity toward a voting system in the policymaking bodies of the Union of States.

"There would be great value," Monnet wrote, "in the evolution together in a single European system of these different types of organizations: a Council of Six Chiefs of Government; Councils of Foreign, Defense and Education Ministers; and the European Economic Communities with their rules, their institutions and their responsibilities. I think that a sort of 'European Confederation' could usefully serve this function. . . .

"I do not doubt, for my part, that a 'Confederation' will lead one day to a 'Federation.' But is it possible to go further at this time? I do not believe so."

As for Britain's bid to participate, Monnet wrote: "Sooner or later, England necessarily must be present. But this presence [must] not slow down the general movement toward European economic and political unity. For example, the participation of Britain must not be limited to political consultations which draw their essential strength from a Common Market in which Britain is not present. . . . The only method . . . is for Britain *first* to take part in the Economic Communities which are the foundation of European union."

This general approach won the support of Germany, Belgium, Italy, and Luxembourg. But the difficult negotiations that ensued among the Six were complicated by Holland. The Dutch advanced what was considered to be the British view: they pressed for Britain's participation in the current negotiations as well as in the ultimate political union itself; they insisted that defense be excluded from the concerns of the Six and left to NATO. Alternatively, in the knowledge that this would block agreement, the Dutch pressed for federal principles that were anathema to de Gaulle—and to the British—and, for this reason, stirred divisions among the Five.

In all, the debate went on for almost two years. Month after month, though often isolated, Dutch Foreign Minister Luns fought a stubborn delaying action. In the end, by insisting there must be either a federal type of union or immediate British participation, he prevented both and helped to bring about what he wanted least, a Franco-German arrangement.

Two Summit meetings of the Six were held in 1961. At the second, in July, de Gaulle made major concessions, and an agreement was reached on the principles of a treaty of political union. Further French concessions were made in the Fouchet Committee's treaty negotiations in the fall, then repudiated in January 1962 when de Gaulle, evidently, read the actual documents for the first time. In the subsequent crisis, de Gaulle flew to Baden Baden in February to see Adenauer and yielded to the main German conditions. He sought to appease Italian resentment at "Franco-German domination" by flying to Turin to see Fanfani. When the Foreign Ministers of the Six met in Paris in April 1962, there was Franco-German agreement on a text. Italy and Luxembourg were more or less prepared to go along.

On April 10, however, Britain made a new move. At a W.E.U. meeting with the Six in Paris, Heath endorsed the political union project in general terms and outlined some of Britain's views. Then, for the first time, he made a direct bid for full British participation in the treaty talks. He proposed that the political negotiations in Paris, which the French and Germans hoped to complete within a few days, and the economic negotiations in Brussels, which had made no progress and were many months from agreement, "go forward together."

On April 17, with Belgian support now, Luns insisted on British participation in the negotiations. And he announced that Holland would refuse to sign the political treaty until Britain had been admitted to the Common Market and could join the political union at the same time. It was a death sentence for what had now become a de Gaulle-Adenauer project.

Adenauer tried to revive the negotiations during his visit to France in July 1962 when, with de Gaulle's agreement, he asked Fanfani to call a Summit meeting of the Six in Rome. The Chancellor was toying with the idea that France, Germany, and Italy might go ahead without the Benelux, if the meeting broke down. Fanfani evaded the issue. He proposed that the Summit be postponed until the Foreign Ministers of the Six had come closer to agreement. No serious attempt to do so was made.

The British denied responsibility for the crack-up. But most of the negotiators for the Six believed the British were behind the Dutch move. It is clear that Dutch resistance could not have continued if Heath, on April 10, had simply withdrawn Britain's objections to a political union of the Six.

The breakdown of the political union talks contributed

heavily to de Gaulle's feeling that Britain was seeking to outmaneuver rather than come to terms with France. All this seemed to the French a preview of how Britain would function after entering the E.E.C. More serious, not only France but three of the Five were thwarted. Their frustration contributed to the disarray that later convinced de Gaulle he could veto Britain without breaking up the Common Market.

Adenauer, particularly, was alienated by Britain's posture on political union. The Chancellor, approaching reluctant retirement, was anxious to crown his twelve-year effort to integrate West Germany into Western Europe. After April 17, 1962, he became less and less enthusiastic about Britain's Common Market bid. A few days later, he suggested publicly that economic "association" with the Common Market might be more appropriate for Britain than full membership, which implied the right to join Europe's projected political union as well. In August 1962, Adenauer lectured his party's Parliamentary Executive about the difficulties that Britain's entry would bring. He predicted trouble for German farming, coal, and textiles. But it was clear that his main concerns were political—the delay in political union, British opposition to federalism, Macmillan's attitude toward Berlin. The Chancellor already was convinced of what de Gaulle told him after one meeting of the French and British leaders: "Macmillan wants to sell out Berlin to the Russians." Adenauer's suspicions about a British deal with Russia had been smoldering since Macmillan's trip to Moscow in 1959. And he told his Parliamentary Executive that there would be a danger, after de Gaulle, of a revival of the old Anglo-French entente against Germany, if Britain entered the Common Market.

In this frame of mind, Adenauer responded enthusiastically when de Gaulle in September 1962 proposed that France and Germany go ahead with a political and military union of their own. It was in the midst of de Gaulle's triumphant tour of Germany. The French President addressed audiences in fluent German and, at one point, revealed that he had a German ancestor. The delirious cheers of giant crowds consecrated the new Bonn-Paris axis.

The plan for a French-German pact failed to shake British and Dutch resistance to a political union of the Six. The Dutch argued privately that the holdup on wider political union would force de Gaulle to admit Britain to the Common Market. It was a serious miscalculation.

De Gaulle's central objective had not been to keep the British out of the Common Market but to weld a political union of the Six before they came in. He saw political union as the route to a common foreign policy which, backed by a common defense, could enable Europe again to play a great-power role in the world. His aim was to shape these European foreign and defense policies before Britain's entry.

This was, in part, what Britain sought to forestall. The British could see that de Gaulle's political-military union, completed without them, would challenge the special British nuclear relationship with the United States. Britain's admission might come to depend on an extremely difficult choice—a choice between American nuclear aid and participation in a European deterrent growing out of a European defense policy. Britain's unfortunate illusion was that it was possible to avoid this choice just as, in the Common Market negotiations, London sought to evade a choice between Europe and the Commonwealth.

There are some who believe that Macmillan would have been prepared to make both difficult choices, in his own time and in his own cautious way. The interaction of domestic and Commonwealth opposition undoubtedly made it difficult for him to come to terms with France rapidly and directly. But speed was of the essence. It is clear now that 1961-62 was the period of opportunity for Britain—an opportunity that Britain missed.

The errors of London were matched by miscalculations in Washington. The United States urged Britain to enter the Common Market. But the political and military implications of that move were only dimly seen. It was little realized that, with or without British entry, events had begun to require a fundamental American accommodation—political and military, as well as economic—with the new Europe and the most vigorous element within it, the France of Charles de Gaulle.

Chapter 7

The U.S. and the New Europe

UNDERLYING the French conflict with the United States and Britain, there has been an ideological dispute about the future of the Atlantic world. De Gaulle wants to move toward a relationship of "two separate but equally powerful entities" between the United States and a uniting Europe. On this—though not on his personal and nationalist ambitions—he has the agreement of most Europeans. The United States, under the Eisenhower administration, and initially under Kennedy, tended to respond to this challenge, if at all, in "Atlantic Community" terms, as did many Britons. What this signified to de Gaulle and a steadily increasing number of Europeans can be seen in the fifteen-nation NATO Council, where all nations theoretically are equal; but one, the United States, is more equal than the others. This structure has meant American leadership or none.

It has meant an alliance where, as de Gaulle sees it, "everything is commanded by the Americans and where the Americans control the use of the principal weapons, that is, atomic arms."

De Gaulle was the first European leader to make this a public issue. But it would be a profound error to believe that he is alone in this view or that this genie can be put back into the bottle.

Nor can de Gaulle's argument be destroyed by accusations that he is seeking to create a "Third Force." De Gaulle's opposition to Communism is as strong as was Kennedy's. If he were one day to engage independent negotiations with Moscow, it would be for reasons parallel to those used by Kennedy to justify his unilateral talks with the Soviets. As one of de Gaulle's cabinet ministers put it recently:

"De Gaulle is not trying to build a Third Force. He is trying to build a Second Force in the West."

Dr. Walter Hallstein, President of the Common Market Commission and hardly a Gaullist, recently asked: "Given a fully united Europe . . . should it be integrated—some would say 'dissolved'—into a so-called 'Atlantic Community' . . . a system which harnesses one giant with a number of comparative dwarfs?" His answer was to propose "a new system" which "joins in partnership . . . twin units which today are already comparable and which one day will be equal," namely the United States and the new Europe.

After eighteen months in office, President Kennedy seemed to accept this concept. At Philadelphia, on July 4,

1962, he spoke of "interdependence" and a "partnership" of "full equality" with Europe. But he was speaking of a distant "goal" to be sought after British entry and a further tightening of Europe's bonds. His speech was filled with such words as "premature" and "some day" and "not built overnight." At no point prior to the Brussels collapse was there a dynamic, imaginative effort to accord progressively equal status immediately to a Europe whose strength and unity, in the White House view, were thought to lie in the somewhat distant future. Yet that is precisely what a majority of Europeans—not de Gaulle alone—wished to see.

The fact is that Washington, as London, simply failed to react in time to the trend. Not until Britain applied to join the Common Market did the United States see itself affected by the new Europe. Even then, the assumption was that there need be no hurry in adjusting the U.S.-European power relationship.

Yet, with or without de Gaulle, the likelihood has always existed that a revived and united Europe, increasingly independent of the United States, one day might go its own way. It was inevitable that the growth of a second Atlantic Giant would crack the mold in which a dominant America had shaped the unity of the West in the post-war period. Before this happened, it was vital for the U.S. and its friends in Europe to find a new structure for unity. It was essential to devise and forge new links of interdependence across the Atlantic more appropriate to the new day.

Foresighted Americans and Europeans such as General Lauris Norstad and Jean Monnet recognized this in the late 'fifties and drew pertinent conclusions. There were voices in Washington and elsewhere which supported their views. But public policy lagged behind.

As early as 1957-58 and again in 1959-60, General Norstad made formal proposals to give the European allies a real voice in the nuclear weapons field. The Eisenhower Administration in its last weeks in office and the Kennedy Administration in 1961 paid lip-service to one aspect of this idea: a NATO multilateral nuclear force. But both Administrations were divided on the issue, and little was done to bring such a force into being. It is ironic now, but as late as December 1962, a few days before Nassau, Secretary of Defense McNamara tried to discourage the project. He told the NATO Ministerial Council that there was no military requirement for a NATO nuclear force.

In this same discourse, McNamara turned inside-out the 1956-57 NATO strategic concept of a "shield" of conventional and tactical nuclear forces, designed to hold briefly, and a strategic nuclear "sword" to defeat the aggressor. He spoke of a nuclear shield, to deter Soviet use of atomic weapons, and a conventional sword to fight the war. He indicated elsewhere that an all-out Soviet conventional attack could be held for three to six months, and even defeated, by stepped-up NATO conventional forces. And he urged the Europeans to satisfy themselves with a conventional role in Atlantic defense. Whether this was good or bad strategic doctrine may be arguable. But it clearly was poor alliance politics. When McNamara took office he found the U.S. Army preparing to fight a two-year war, while the U.S. Air Force was prepared for a war of a few weeks. A new, unified strategic doctrine for the U.S. Armed Forces undoubtedly was necessary. But the day had long since passed when a strategy made in Washington without consulting the Allies could be imposed on Europe.

Some elements of the Administration sought a different approach. In March 1961, Dean Acheson spoke to General de Gaulle of his plan for a NATO nuclear force controlled by a five-nation "war cabinet." He gave de Gaulle the impression that there would be no single-nation veto, for he indicated that the European elements would be able to commit the U.S. Strategic Air Command by striking alone, if necessary. But despite other, similar hints, the issue of the veto was never clarified. Later, de Gaulle was accused of building a small independent deterrent to "trigger" American nuclear strength.

In September 1962, White House Security Advisor Mc-George Bundy went so far as to suggest that the United States, under certain conditions, would accept, within NATO, a European nuclear force in which the U.S. neither would participate nor possess a veto. But the central thrust of U.S. policy before January 1963 remained the opposite of sharing nuclear responsibility with Europe. It was a policy of maintaining the American nuclear monopoly— with a British appendage that, it was hoped, would ultimately disappear.

In the economic field, Jean Monnet launched the concept of "partnership" with the United States as early as 1957 and, more precisely, in June 1959, shortly after the Common Market began to function. The West-European nations, he said then, "no longer dependents . . . are ready for the full responsibilities of partnership." For this "new era" he urged a "new Atlantic initiative" to face "new problems common both to Europe and America."

"The creation of the Common Market," Monnet said, "has already had substantial repercussions in non-member countries. These repercussions are likely to increase rather than diminish." The Common Market Six, he pointed out, "are on the way to establishing new political arrangements under which policies as well as resources will be merged."

"A new institutional approach is necessary," Monnet said, to "concert policies" among "the *major* Western industrial powers on both sides of the Atlantic" in a limited number of critical fields: monetary stability, economic growth, aid to underdeveloped areas and world commodity stabilization as well as tariff arrangements. "What is at stake," said the Action Committee for a United States of Europe, "is no longer simply the question of how trade problems should be settled . . . but rather how to solve the economic problems facing all the countries of the West, including the United States."

Monnet's chief objective was one which the Common Market Commission endorsed in its First Memorandum in February 1959. It was, as the Commission put it, nothing less than to bring together for "joint action" the "three great units" which are "the motive force of the economy of the free world: the United States, the United Kingdom and the [European] Community." It was an objective that preceded Britain's application to join the Common Market. It has increased pertinence now, after the failure of Britain's Brussels bid.

Monnet's proposal was taken up by Douglas Dillon, then the U.S. Undersecretary of State. It led in 1960 to the reorganization of the eighteen-nation O.E.E.C. as the twenty-nation Organization for Economic Cooperation and Development (OECD), with the U.S. and Canada joining the Europeans as full members. But the OECD, despite some useful work, has failed to perform the essential tasks for which it was conceived. The reasons for failure include a weak secretariat, a too-numerous membership and a loose charter. Two key elements suggested by Monnet were missing: the Six refused to sit as a Community, acting as one; and a small policy council to bring the U.S., Britain, and the Common Market together for joint decisions was never set up. But, above all, what the OECD has lacked has been a mandate for action. The weak O.E.E.C. charter, which permitted binding decisions only by unanimity, was watered down further to satisfy the United States: the OECD was not authorized to make binding decisions at all; it can only consult and recommend.

The chief American negotiator in creating OECD, Ambassador John Tuthill, made this public comment in the spring of 1963 about OECD consultation: "The United States Government, in my view, was slow in concluding that this type of consultation was needed. Even (in 1960) in the negotiation for the establishment of the OECD, there remained skeptics in certain parts of our government who questioned whether we should consult in this intimate fashion on such highly sensitive issues as policies in agriculture, finance, economic growth, etc."

Tuthill went on to say that the Kennedy Administration, unlike the Eisenhower Administration, had no hesitancy about consultation. And this was true. The New Frontier sought to use the OECD machinery to influence European monetary, economic, and foreign-aid policy. It even sought European recommendations to influence the U. S. Congress. It was willing to talk about international programs for stabilization of agricultural and other commodities, something that was anathema to the Eisenhower cabinet. But talk can only be a first step. Except in one important instance, the Kennedy Administration prior to January 1963 held back from real partnership, the kind that involves action and a sharing both of responsibility and the power of decision. This single instance occurred in the monetary field.

In January 1961, Jean Monnet saw in the continuing U.S. dollar crisis a mounting threat to the West and an opportunity to advance Atlantic unity. A spectacular run from the dollar in the fall of 1960 had lifted U.S. gold losses to an annual rate of $6 billion. In an interview with this writer in *U.S. News & World Report,* Monnet urged "a joint approach by the Governments of Europe, including Britain, in partnership with the United States" to strengthen confidence in the dollar and to "stabilize the currencies of the West."

What should be done—many national and international

techniques had been advanced in the preceding year or two by monetary experts—seemed less important to Monnet than *who* could do it effectively. He added:

> While we must examine solutions involving the International Monetary Fund, we should as a first step think of what we can do quickly to the same ends by reinforcing the partnership of Europe and America. . . .
>
> The principal actors in the monetary dramas of recent years have been the U.S., Britain, the Common Market countries, Switzerland and Canada. While gold reserves have shifted back and forth among these countries, they always have had almost nine-tenths of the gold of the non-Communist world. By acting together, these countries have the power to put the free world's monetary system on a sound and stable basis. . . .
>
> During and after the war, gold flowed from Europe to the U.S. We had the famous 'dollar gap' that was closed by the Marshall Plan. Now the flow is in the other direction. One day, it could easily be reversed again.
>
> It should be possible to solve these problems without periodically endangering the whole economic structure of the West. We need permanent machinery that will enable the U.S. and Europe to cooperate in this field on a continuous, rather than a crisis, basis.

The Kennedy Administration discussed this problem with its Atlantic allies in the nine-nation OECD monetary committee. But it sought action in another forum—the sixty-seven-nation International Monetary Fund, which was dominated by the U.S. and Britain. The U.S. proposed that the continental European countries make some $3 billion of their currencies available to the I.M.F. in the form of stand-by credits. It amounted to a doubling of the European currency in the Fund upon which the U.S. could draw, if necessary. The U.S., Britain, and Canada were also to pledge about $3 billion in their own currencies for reverse circumstances. But it was not expected that these funds would be used in any immediate future.

The key issue, argued out during the I.M.F. conference in Vienna in September 1961, was whether the I.M.F. or the lending countries would decide on use of the new reserves. The U.S., as the chief prospective borrower, wanted something close to automatic drawing rights under normal I.M.F. procedures. Most of the Common Market countries —with little voting strength in the I.M.F.—insisted on a wide range of safeguards, including consultation before their currencies were drawn out. French Finance Minister Wilfrid Baumgartner—a long-time Governor of the Bank of France and no Gaullist; he left the French Government a few months later—demanded a veto. He insisted that "each country should remain judge . . . of the use of its own currency."

The compromise agreement that was reached took the route Monnet had proposed eight months earlier. It provided for I.M.F. machinery to handle the mechanics. But the decision on each drawing of funds was made the multilateral responsibility of the ten nations contributing to the new reserves. France yielded on the veto. The U.S. yielded on automaticity. It was agreed that decisions by the new ten-nation "Paris Club" could be made by qualified majority votes—the votes of seven countries which had contributed sixty per cent of the new reserves. In effect, the agreement was a step toward a limited kind of Atlantic reserve fund. And the same countries, meeting in the OECD monetary committee, thus acquired an incentive for day-to-day co-operation by Finance Ministries and central banks that subsequently gave OECD its only significant continuing success.

Most important, an *ad hoc* Atlantic institution had been created with decision-making machinery that, for the first time, reflected the new balance of financial power in the West. Sovereignty had been pooled in a way new to the Atlantic area.

This beginning in true Atlantic partnership could have set a precedent for action on other critical economic problems as well as more permanent monetary reform. Further steps toward an Atlantic reserve fund, for example, could have strengthened the dollar and pound, forced the pace toward joint business-cycle policy and stimulated common policies for balanced economic growth on both sides of the Atlantic. But the precedent of the "Paris Club" was not followed up in any field, not even in the field of stopgap monetary measures. In building further short-term defenses for the dollar, U.S. Undersecretary of the Treasury Robert Roosa sought bilateral deals with European countries individually through swap arrangements and sales of U.S. Treasury obligations. He opposed new machinery to deal on a permanent basis with the long-term "liquidity" problem.

The main thrust of U.S. policy in the Atlantic economic field turned in October 1961 toward the Trade Expansion

Act—a measure that skirted the central issue posed by Europe's union and aroused some suspicion of America's aims.

THE Trade Expansion Act repeated, five years later, one of the errors Britain had made in its initial reaction to the Common Market. To many Europeans, Washington's plan looked like London's Free Trade Area scheme in another and even broader form.

There was an important difference, which America's friends recognized but Gaullists and some others ignored. The British in 1956-58 sought to dissolve the Common Market in a wider commercial grouping, a move that would have destroyed the burgeoning economic and political union of the Six. Washington had favored Europe's union and had encouraged Britain to join; the Trade Expansion Act was an attempt initially to limit the trade damages to the U.S. and, later, to achieve increased exchanges. Freer trade, it was hoped, would open the way toward cooperation in other fields. But the timing of the measure was bad. And one provision—authorizing zero tariffs—cast a shadow over a project that, otherwise, might have been well received.

Undersecretary of State George Ball evidently suspected it was a mistake to rush trade legislation on the heels of Britain's Common Market bid. A well-informed observer, writing early in 1962, reported that "The Ball Group . . . was concerned lest precipitate American action in 1962 complicate the entry of Britain into the Common Market. To gain time, it favored letting the 1958 Trade Act expire, and then writing a new bill for submission to a new Congress in 1963." (*The Grand Design,* by Joseph Kraft.)

But when the President ruled otherwise, even Ball was surprised at the nature of Europe's reaction. The Europeans welcomed plans to negotiate toward a fifty percent reciprocal tariff cut. They were pleased at the turn away from escape clauses and peril points. They found, in the plans for adjustment assistance, an Administration intention to reduce tariffs even when it hurt. But all this got less attention than the provisions permitting zero tariffs on products in which the U.S. and the Common Market conducted eighty percent of world trade. That provision would have covered a large part of U.S.-European trade in manufactured goods, if Britain had entered the Common Market.

To Europeans this seemed like an attempt to create an Atlantic Free Trade Area, wiping out much of the Common Market's external tariff. The external tariff was considered one of the vital elements in unifying the economies of the member countries over the next decade.

Ball hastened to Europe to reassure Common Market leaders. He said that the Administration had merely sought the widest possible bargaining authority. He argued that most-favored-nation treatment would extend the tariff cuts to the whole world, proving that there was no thought of an Atlantic free-trade area.

But with zero tariffs projected for products traded most heavily in the Atlantic area, many Europeans were not convinced. Some suspected a fine British hand had been involved in shaping that part of the Trade Act; French diplomats in Washington reported that the initial draft had been "written in the British Embassy." There was fear that West Germany and Holland would be tempted by Atlantic zero tariffs as they had been by the European zero tariffs in Britain's free-trade-area scheme.

Suspicions about an Atlantic free-trade area, fed further by Britain's sponsorship of the EFTA countries, played an important part in de Gaulle's decision to veto British entry into the Common Market. And it was one reason why many of the Europeans who detested the way de Gaulle excluded Britain nevertheless felt a sense of relief that the negotiations had ended.

Oddly enough, Europe's opposition to the zero-tariff clause was little grasped in the United States. So well-informed a Congressman as Representative Henry Reuss of Wisconsin remained convinced, even after de Gaulle's veto, that the zero tariff provision was an incentive to the Common Market to admit Britain.

A FUNDAMENTAL error in comprehension in the United States was reflected in the Trade Expansion Act, which absorbed the Administration's energies for a year. Many in Washington evidently were bemused by the words "common market" and overlooked the true meaning and real title of the European Economic Community. The six nations of the new Europe were reducing their tariffs for each other not primarily as a means of increasing trade but as a step toward "a more perfect union."

"We're not in business; we're in politics." This widely

quoted remark by Dr. Walter Hallstein should have pointed to the overriding objective of the new Europe. That objective was never simply a customs union, but a political union, first in the economic field. The contribution of Jean Monnet to the second half of the twentieth century was not a new trade scheme but a method of uniting nations. The Europeans recognized the legitimate American interest in reciprocal tariff reductions and were willing to go along—up to a point. But their real interest in relations with the United States lay elsewhere.

The essential political nature of Europe's union required a political response from the United States. That response had to face up to the new power balance developing in the West. It had to envisage a transformation of outmoded Atlantic patterns. It had to recognize the inevitable evolution toward a new relationship—"a relationship of two separate but equally powerful entities." Whatever the nostalgia for a bygone day, the U.S. had to realize that there was no future in "Atlantic Community" proposals which would disguise but maintain American rather than joint U.S.-European leadership.

Nothing has been more misleading since January 1963 than the general belief in the U.S. and Britain that the Common Market, under French influence, is seeking an "inward-looking" Europe. Vested interests may lead France to resist large tariff cuts on industrial products; German farmers may cling to high prices and protection. But the essential orientation of the Six is "outward-looking" in the sense that continental Europe is determined to play a more important role in the world. And this is at least as true of Gaullist France as it is of any of the other countries.

In his early months in office, President Kennedy admitted that "no one nation has the power or the wisdom to solve all the problems of the world or manage all its revolutionary tides." He later said repeatedly that the U.S. no longer could carry world-wide defense and aid burdens alone. Nor has the U.S. alone been able to solve the West's increasingly dangerous problems of monetary instability, farm surpluses, lagging growth rates, booms and slumps and declines in world commodity prices. Such declines in recent years—the result of a too-free market—have seen the industrial countries mulct the underdeveloped exporting nations of far more than they have given back in the form of grants-in-aid.

If the United States wanted Europe's help in such fields, it should have begun by proposing *ad hoc* institutions for these purposes in which Europe could have had an equal voice on the board.

A real burden-sharing partnership is impossible between one great power and numerous smaller nations, as in NATO, or on a bilateral basis. In such a relationship, the Giant necessarily calls the tune—or fails to lead—and no one else can take its place. The others inevitably become submissive or resentful and, in any case, cannot assume responsibility. Whatever effort a small nation may make, its added contribution is bound to be so limited compared to the total that there is little incentive to sacrifice. This can be changed only by the uniting of Europe. As the new Europe senses its ability to influence events on the American scale, it will want to do so. That already is beginning to happen. But it cannot take the form of a European contribution to projects shaped in Washington. Either the strategy of the West will be shaped jointly by the U.S. and Europe in the political, economic, and military fields, or Europe ultimately will shape its own.

On December 6, 1961, in announcing his coming foreign trade program, President Kennedy said: "This is not speculation about some grand design for the future." And, in the mind of the President, it seems clear, there was no **Grand Design** at that time, whatever thoughts others below him may have had.

In May 1962, the *London Times* reported this quip by Dean Acheson about the so-called Grand Design: It "comes from the Press Club bar. Walt Rostow [State Department director of policy planning] has inherited a project of trying to write down everything that has gone on and trying to tie it together. I believe the psychiatrists call this rationalization."

In the spring of 1962, a visitor told one of the President's closest advisers of Europe's skepticism about the Trade Act. Many Europeans, he said, felt the United States was interested in protecting American trade, but not in sharing power with Europe.

"They may be right," smiled the White House adviser.

But on July 4, 1962, President Kennedy said: "We believe that a united Europe will be capable of playing a greater role in the common defense, of responding more generously to the needs of poorer nations, of joining with the United States and others in lowering trade barriers, resolving problems of commerce and commodities and currency, and developing coordinated policies in all economic, political and diplomatic areas. We see in such a Europe a partner with whom we can deal on a basis of full equality in all the great and burdensome tasks of building and defending a community of free nations."

This was a Grand Design.

Yet, prior to January 1963, the United States still failed to face up to the implications of the united Europe—of the Six—that already was taking shape. President Kennedy had begun by seeking to restore American leadership at a time, in 1961, when a clear need already had arisen for common action and joint leadership with Europe. When this need finally was seen, its urgency was overlooked; action was delayed pending Britain's entry, mortgaging U.S. policy to London's dilatory methods. And, all this time, the Atlantic solidarity upon which partnership had to be based repeatedly was strained by the pursuit of other, conflicting objectives —felt to be of overriding importance—such as maintenance of the U.S. nuclear monopoly in the West and unilateral negotiations with Russia.

Chapter 8

A Policy for Atlantic Partnership

IT IS TOO late to repair the errors of the past. But it is not too soon to shape a policy for the future. Not much help can be expected from London in this. The British are still caught up in their post-Brussels confusion, intensified by a national political scandal and a divisive electoral campaign. That is all the more reason for others, particularly the U.S., to set a clear course. And, in this, the past can be a guide. While there have been important developments since January 1963—none more important than the tragic assassination of John F. Kennedy and his replacement by Lyndon B. Johnson—most of the underlying factors remain the same:

(1) The Common Market of the Six is still a going concern. It is the only united Europe that exists or will exist for some time. There has been less Community spirit since de Gaulle's veto of Britain and more emphasis on reciproc-

ity in national concessions. But forward movement has gone on and is likely to continue, despite predictable difficulties for 1964 over grain prices and tariff negotiations with the United States. A great thrust ahead was made as 1963 ended. Through a Franco-German compromise, the mainly industrial European Economic Community was extended to most of agriculture—averting a serious crisis over de Gaulle's July warning that otherwise the Common Market might "disappear." It is probable that this critical step now has made Europe's economic union—to use Jean Monnet's expression—"irreversible." All plans for the West must start from these facts of life.

(2) Political union of the Six is still on the agenda, and negotiations may be resumed actively in 1964. Before 1963 was over, Chancellor Erhard of Germany and Foreign Minister Spaak of Belgium urged a new initiative on de Gaulle. And the French President in his year-end speech listed, as his most important task abroad in 1964, "the union of Europe . . . in the domains of politics, defense and culture as . . . in that of economics." When political union comes, it may be more federal in nature than the loose "Union of States" proposed by the Fouchet Plan. Pressure for a federal union is such, from the Five and within France, that de Gaulle's Prime Minister and his Foreign Minister now have been forced to pay lip service to "federation" rather than "confederation" as the ultimate goal. In the economic sphere, the fusion of the executive commissions of the three existing European Communities—to which France agreed in principle at the end of 1963—will consolidate and thus

enhance the powers of the most vigorous federal institutions of the new Europe.

(3) British entry into the Common Market is off the agenda, probably for several years. Prime Minister Sir Alec Douglas-Home favors entry, but some of the most important Conservative Party leaders remain reluctant. The Labor Party, which seems headed for power, is opposed. French terms for British entry have been raised since January 1963. A defense deal in the nuclear missile field is now the central condition and is likely to remain so as long as de Gaulle is in power. It can be undercut, if at all, only by a British proposal to participate in an integrated European deterrent— a proposal Jean Monnet unsuccessfully urged London to make during the January 1963 crisis. Despite some high-level backing, both the Conservatives and the Laborites still oppose that now. Nor are the Continental Five, in the present state of British opinion, overly enthusiastic about immediate British entry into the Common Market; they have insisted on continued "contacts" with Britain primarily as a means of keeping the heat on the French.

(4) U.S. negotiations with Russia face less opposition from Germany with Adenauer's departure from the Chancellorship. Though substantial elements of the Christian Democratic Party remain hostile to East-West talks, there is a majority in all three German parties now for careful contact with Moscow—if there is advance agreement on objectives. Fear of a U.S.-Soviet deal at Germany's expense continues, as was demonstrated by the West German reaction to the nuclear test-ban treaty in the summer of 1963. But the

Bonn Government under Chancellor Erhard and Foreign Minister Schroeder no longer is relying primarily on the French to influence the U.S. and Britain. It is advancing its own views, becoming a subject as well as an object in international relations. And the United States now seems prepared to accept this. Since the Spring of 1963, Washington has made a point of informing and consulting the Germans continuously. It has become clear, even to Khrushchev, that there can be no Berlin, German, or European settlement without West German acquiescence.

(5) The U.S.-French dispute over NATO and nuclear weapons has entered a new phase. After the test-ban agreement in July 1963, President Kennedy for the first time recognized France as a nuclear power under the Atomic Energy Act. That meant new legislation no longer would be needed to grant France nuclear assistance similar to that given Britain. In a July 25 letter to de Gaulle and in his August 1 press conference, the President mentioned three conditions for U.S. aid. He wanted France to sign the test-ban treaty and to halt atmospheric testing; to come to agreement on "the organization of the defense of the West"; and to join in "a cooperative effort" to satisfy the desires of West Germany and other non-nuclear NATO countries for participation in the West's nuclear deterrent. He also pointed out that Britain, in return for Polaris, had agreed at Nassau to place its V-bombers and its future Polaris force "under NATO." De Gaulle replied on August 2 that he intended to continue testing, presumably until the French H-bomb is developed in 1966-67. He said he would make no arrange-

ments that would deprive the French deterrent of its independence. But he did not close the door on the offer. While neither side was prepared to move further immediately, it became clear to both that for the first time the way was open for a serious Franco-American discussion on defense. An indication that de Gaulle was responding to the new atmosphere came in October 1963 when Couve de Murville, visiting Washington, told Kennedy that the French President had no further plans to reduce cooperation with NATO.

There have been other indications, as well, that a new flexibility might emerge in Paris. Events, for example, were moving strongly toward resumption of a Franco-American dialogue during the last months of the Kennedy Administration. This trend was interrupted by the Dallas assassination. But the underlying circumstances are unlikely to change, and they deserve examination.

During most of 1963, in the wake of the French veto, circumstances evolved unfavorably for Gaullist policy. Although the French President had his defenders in Europe, he was generally blamed for the way Britain was excluded, for the continued strain in French relations with the U.S. and NATO, and for the slowdown in progress toward European union. French ties with Bonn failed to develop as effectively as the General had hoped when he signed the Franco-German Treaty with Adenauer; even before Erhard became Chancellor, the West Germans increasingly showed a mind of their own. Closer relations between Bonn and Washington, actively sought by Kennedy, led de Gaulle's cabinet ministers to talk with concern about the danger of Franco-American "competition" for German loyalty. Instead of achieving the leadership of Europe, aided by German backing, the General found himself threatened with isolation within Europe and within the Atlantic world.

At the same time, the French President became concerned lest the improvement in Anglo-American relations with Russia, stemming from the test-ban treaty, lead to a deal over Germany in his absence—"another Yalta," his aides called it. With the West Germans participating in Western planning for talks with Moscow, de Gaulle began to feel that the French policy of total "non-participation" had outworn its usefulness. All these factors placed the General under pressure to re-enter the Anglo-American dialogue with Russia and to improve relations with the United States—steps that Bonn, particularly, urged upon him, as did many of his own officials.

De Gaulle's dilemma was that he remained as opposed as ever to negotiations with Russia on Berlin and Germany. The status quo—the de facto division of Germany—suited him very well; he saw no advantage for France in moves either toward legalizing the division or ending it. Moves toward reunification would present France with the prospect of a nation of eighty million Germans on its eastern frontier. Moves toward legal acceptance by the West of Germany's division increased the danger that Germans ultimately would look toward Moscow to reunite their country. One day, de Gaulle predicted, a Russia in trouble might become willing to make major concessions to a united West Europe. Until that distant day, the status quo would remain, for France, the best of all possible worlds.

De Gaulle saw his task, therefore, as one of re-entering the Western dialogue with Russia, if he could steer it away from the German problem. His strategy, he indicated in July 1963, was to return to the world stage before the end of the year by summoning a disarmament conference of the "four nuclear powers" in Paris. But this proposal received an unfavorable response and de Gaulle, a few months later, was forced temporarily to shelve it.

Meanwhile, the French President began to yield to the necessity of renewed contact with the United States. He had refused to invite Kennedy to Paris during the President's European tour in June 1963—a tour designed, de Gaulle felt, to organize Europe against him. But Kennedy's continued efforts to arrange a meeting intensified the French and European pressure on de Gaulle to patch up relations with Washington. De Gaulle responded initially by sending his Foreign Minister to see Kennedy in May and October 1963. And during the latter meeting, Couve de Murville let it be known that the General would cross the Atlantic for a "working visit" with Kennedy early in 1964.

On November 20, only two days before his death, Kennedy discussed the projected visit with French Ambassador Hervé Alphand. De Gaulle was prepared to spend a working weekend at Hyannisport in March, a time when he expected the first Mirage IV unit of his "Force de Frappe" to become operational. The only remaining detail to be settled was whether or not de Gaulle would rescind his refusal to spend an additional day in Washington, as Kennedy urged. Kennedy told Alphand he wanted to stage a parade "to prove to the General that he is the most popular and respected foreign dignitary in the United States."

It is impossible to predict now what would have happened if this meeting—the first between the two Presidents in almost three years—could have taken place. Kennedy certainly had no illusions that one meeting could resolve the fundamental French conflicts with the United States, Europe, or NATO. He suspected that de Gaulle preferred for his own reasons to maintain tension between Washington and Paris. And he felt sure, as he told visitors, that the General did not want "an intimate relationship" with the United States. But there was an obvious need, after such a long lapse, to resume personal contact. And a beginning might have been made toward restoring a working arrangement between the two countries.

In one area of disagreement, the swift pace of technology had created a political opportunity that Kennedy was preparing to exploit. The Atomic Energy Commission in 1963 had achieved a breakthrough in underground nuclear testing, the only kind still permitted by the treaty with Russia banning tests in the atmosphere, under water, and in outer space. The A.E.C. earlier had been convinced that nothing substantially larger than the 20-kiloton Hiroshima bomb could be exploded subterraneously. But prodding from the White House led A.E.C. technicians to drill and emplace their test-bombs ever deeper into the earth. By the Fall of

1963, it had become clear that thermonuclear blasts of about a megaton could be contained without surface eruption. By extrapolation, the data could even serve to replace tests of H-bombs many times larger.

Kennedy planned, when he met de Gaulle, to offer this know-how to the General in return for French signature of the test-ban treaty. Hints of this, meanwhile, were given to French officials. Such aid, it was evident, would save France the great expense and opprobrium involved in atmospheric testing of H-bombs in the Pacific. And it promised to eliminate a major source of contention not only between Paris and Washington, but between Paris and Moscow as well.

The Dallas assassination interrupted this hopeful evolution in Franco-American relations. The French President came to Washington for the Kennedy funeral and a few hours later had his first brief meeting—and first misunderstanding—with President Johnson. The 22-minute talk gave Johnson the impression, which he then announced publicly to some thirty American Governors, that de Gaulle had reconfirmed his agreement to visit the United States early in 1964. Within forty-eight hours, de Gaulle let it be known officially that he too felt a "thorough examination" of Franco-American differences was essential in 1964. But he wanted Johnson to come to Paris for their first substantive talk—as had Presidents Eisenhower and Kennedy and all of Europe's important leaders, except Chancellor Adenauer. Adenauer's reluctance in 1958 led to a meeting half-way between Bonn and Paris, but still on French soil, at de Gaulle's country home.

Early in December 1963, Johnson sent de Gaulle a note thanking him for coming to the Kennedy funeral, and he added: "I look for more thorough conversations with you next year." But, at the same time, he indicated at a news conference that he could not leave the country before the 1964 elections. He made the same response in January 1964 when the French Ambassador, on instructions, suggested a compromise—a meeting "half-way," on the French Caribbean island of Martinique during de Gaulle's projected trip to Mexico in March. While events could change the outlook, Johnson's unwillingness to go to Martinique made a meeting before 1965 unlikely.

Whether the U. S. and French Presidents confer in 1964 or in 1965 is less important than what they talk about when they meet. It will be vital to avoid one pitfall—the illusion, widely held, that significant French cooperation can be obtained in exchange for U.S. nuclear assistance. Nuclear aid is something de Gaulle personally never has asked, although he has permitted his Ministers and Generals to do so. De Gaulle has hinted privately that he prefers France to build its own deterrent. He has assumed a "Don't-tempt-me" posture by saying that if he were the American President, he would not offer nuclear aid to a French national force. The truth is that de Gaulle fears he might compromise his freedom in an American nuclear embrace. As a result, he is not prepared to concede much for U. S. aid, although he is under considerable pressure from his cabinet and the French military to seek it. That being so, it would hardly be wise for the U.S. to trade away this valuable

American asset for a few meaningless gestures. A much broader negotiation is indicated. Far more, for example, might be achieved by authorizing British nuclear cooperation with France—something de Gaulle has sought and wants—under conditions that would protect the general Western interest. One such condition could be a requirement that the British and French organize, and provide warheads for, an integrated European force open to others and co-ordinated with the United States—a force that could replace or later grow out of the projected NATO multilateral Polaris fleet that now is being planned with American, but without French, participation. There are important French and British cabinet ministers who have discussed similar ideas. They believe this approach could open the door for British entry into the Common Market and that it would accelerate the political union of Europe. A lesser result would scarcely warrant rewarding de Gaulle with nuclear aid. But nuclear aid alone, in this writer's opinion, will not be enough to extract significant cooperation from the General.

In relations with the United States, de Gaulle's primary objective has always been, and remains, not nuclear assistance, but policy coordination that enhances French and European influence in the world. This was the condition for French cooperation with NATO that de Gaulle laid down in his September 1958 memorandum to Eisenhower and Macmillan; when it was denied, he withdrew his Mediterranean Fleet from NATO and refused to permit nuclear stockpiles for U.S. fighter-bombers and missiles on French soil. Global policy coordination remains, in a somewhat different form, de Gaulle's objective today. The General has shelved, for the time being, his old idea of a tripartite U.S.-British-French "directorate" to undertake global decision-making for the Atlantic Alliance. The Franco-German Treaty now makes it difficult for him to exclude Bonn from any new formal arrangement. Nor is de Gaulle any longer making extravagant claims for a veto over U.S. use of nuclear weapons anywhere in the world; he simply insists that he will not commit all his conventional and nuclear forces to NATO while the U.S. keeps its most powerful forces outside Alliance control. The General's immediate aims are to "complete" the economic union of Europe—by extending it fully to agriculture—and to resume his efforts for a political "Union of States." As for the United States, his proposal is to "concert" policy issue by issue and to "coordinate" nuclear strategy. In this, he hopes one day to be able to speak for a united Europe.

The French President re-stated his chief objectives as follows in his 1963 year-end speech:

"France, because she can do so, because she is France, should conduct amidst the world a world policy. . . . We must assist our Western Europe, from the time that it is united, in practicing with America a truly concerted political, economic and strategic entente."

This offer of a political and economic, as well as a strategic, "entente" is de Gaulle's first public response to the long-building pressure on both sides of the Atlantic, and particularly from Bonn, for a French commitment to the concept of U.S.-European partnership. And, as such, it warrants thorough exploration. But attempts to concert policy are unlikely to get very far by themselves.

If the United States wants de Gaulle's cooperation, it will have to cater to the prestige of France—directly and through the person of its President. Some cooperation could be obtained cheaply that way. Prestige is important to the General. He considers it "the mainspring" of leadership; and leadership of Europe is one of his central aims. French leadership in Europe could be as much in the U.S. interest now as it was a decade ago when Washington encouraged it actively. It is something the U.S. should be prepared to support, if it is a leadership of the first among equals, not a cover for domination, and if there is a clear understanding in advance as to where Europe will be led. Under these conditions, the West Germans would be prepared to go along. The new German leaders want friendship with France, their channel to unity with West Europe, as well as a close alliance with the United States, their military protector. They do not want to choose between Paris and Washington. On the contrary, it is in their interest to bring the U.S. and France together, and they would be prepared to do a great deal toward this end.

NONE OF THIS means that Washington must surrender to Gaullist ambitions that run counter to the interests of the West as a whole. While Britain must come to terms with France before it can come to terms with Europe, the U.S. has broader options. What must be elaborated in a prolonged dialogue with de Gaulle—and with other Europeans—is a framework for a U.S. partnership with the new Europe, not with France alone. Important as de Gaulle may be in the European configuration, it would be as dangerous to focus too much on his role as it would be to think he can be ignored.

Relations with the General will never be easy. The French President carries old scars and suspicions from his wartime experience with Britain and the United States. His new attachment to Europe is as nationalistic as his continued attachment to France. Had it not been for de Gaulle's veto, it is likely that Britain would be in the Common Market now. Without a doubt, de Gaulle was and remains an obstacle to real federal union in Europe, to an integrated defense in NATO and to a partnership of mutual confidence with the United States. But an obstacle is not the same as an immovable roadblock. We must not be misled by the understandable temptation to blame all the current difficulties on de Gaulle's obstruction. We must not overlook what the United States and its friends in Europe failed to do in the past—and need to do in the future—to organize the West, whether or not de Gaulle is in office.

As we have seen, de Gaulle for a time was prepared to accept British entry into the Common Market. Prior to November 1962, a French veto was impossible in any case. It became possible as a result of Britain's dilatory tactics, a surprise political upset in France, and disarray among the Five—including, particularly, the defection of Adenauer. Errors by Britain, the United States, and their friends in Europe contributed to that disarray and provided de Gaulle with added incentives, plus a pretext, for his destructive "Non!" At the end, a last-minute opportunity at Nassau to reverse de Gaulle's decision was missed.

Britain contributed to its own defeat first by resisting economic, then political union of the Six and later by clinging to Commonwealth preferences, to its EFTA allies, to its special relationship with the United States, and to its unique agricultural system.

The United States came late to its Grand Design and, prior to de Gaulle's press conference, saw no need to act vigorously to implement it. Whether or not everything should have been hinged on British entry into the Common Market can be argued. But it certainly was unwise to leave the development of America's relations with a uniting Europe so completely and so long in the hands of the negotiators of another country.

What was chiefly lacking in Washington, prior to January 1963, was something de Gaulle once described as "that organic whole of continuous plans, matured decisions and measures carried to their conclusion, which we call a policy" —a policy to bring the Grand Design about. No lesson of the January crisis was more important than that.

THE SETBACK to Atlantic Partnership in January 1963 forced some hard thinking on both sides of the ocean. The results have not been unhopeful. Nor do prospects for the future warrant pessimism.

Disarray among the Common Market Five is largely a thing of the past. As early as the Spring of 1963, the debate in the West German Bundestag on the Franco-German Treaty showed Adenauer isolated even before his withdrawal from office. Government and opposition parties united on a preamble that ruled out key Gaullist policies. It assured German backing for federal union in Europe, integration in NATO, liberal trade programs and partnership with the United States. Adenauer's retirement now has deprived de Gaulle of his only real ally.

Looking a bit ahead, the Third Stage of the Common Market in January 1966 will bring qualified majority voting on agriculture, tariffs and other subjects. It will deprive France of its veto in these fields. At about the same time, and perhaps somewhat sooner, Presidential elections in France should begin to unfreeze the French political situation. The Gaullist U.N.R. will need allies by then, if by some chance de Gaulle does not run; they will need them a year later, in any case, for Parliamentary elections. Concessions in foreign policy are likely: the only possible allies are firm advocates of European federal union and Atlantic Partnership. All favor an integrated, multilateral European deterrent—or an Atlantic deterrent without a U.S. veto—rather than a French national nuclear force. De Gaulle's own Prime Minister believes a European deterrent will be an ultimate necessity—and that it must be based on a Franco-British, not a Franco-German core. His Defense and Foreign Ministers already have paid lip-service publicly to the European-deterrent idea.

The most hopeful signs since January 1963 have been those indicating that Washington finally was beginning to shape a policy for the West and was seeking ways to implement it. Whether or not it devised the best tactics at the start is a matter of lesser importance. Tactics always can change. But the multilateral nuclear force proposal, the Herter mission to Geneva, President Kennedy's enormously successful trip to Germany, and his advocacy of Atlantic monetary reform—which brought about a study by the 10-nation "Paris Club"—all indicated a determination to come to grips with the problems posed by Europe's revival. All these initiatives now are being pressed forward by President Johnson.

The direction American policy must continue to take was set forth clearly and unmistakably in Kennedy's Paulskirche speech in Frankfurt on June 25, 1963.

"We look forward," he said, "to a Europe united and strong . . . a world power capable of meeting world problems as a full and equal partner . . . a fully cohesive Europe that can protect us all against fragmentation of our alliance. With only such a Europe can we have a full give-and-take between equals, an equal sharing of responsibility and an equal level of sacrifice . . . the choice of the paths to the unity of Europe is a choice Europeans must take. But . . . you should know that this new European greatness will not be an object of fear, but a source of strength, for the United States of America."

Atlantic Partnership, the President said, is "the future of the West . . . It will be achieved by concrete steps to solve the problems that face us all: military, economic and political. Partnership is not a posture but a process." He called for "common industrial and agricultural policies across the Atlantic . . . to give new impetus to growth." He proposed commodity-stabilization agreements and Atlantic monetary reform: "The great free nations of the world must take control of our monetary problems if these problems are not to take control of us."

The President hinted that the American veto would not be permanent in the proposed NATO multilateral nuclear force. "As Europe moves toward unity," he said, "its role and responsibility, here as elsewhere, would and must increase accordingly."

In negotiations with Russia, he said, "we will not bargain one nation's interest against another." And while speaking of a "sharing of power" with Europe, he restated the American military commitment to the old world in these terms: "The United States will risk its cities to defend your freedom because we need your freedom to protect ours."

This dramatic Kennedy speech was drafted in consultation with Jean Monnet, who came to Washington for the purpose. From it, as from the whole context of the Kennedy trip to Germany, there emerged clearly the revised Kennedy strategy that President Johnson now is pursuing in Europe. That strategy leaves the door open for a dialogue with de Gaulle. But it concentrates on "shaping the inevitable" for the French President. It is a strategy based on two fundamentals.

First, there is the effort to restore a relationship of confidence with West Germany, an effort that Kennedy launched in June and that Johnson effectively continued in his December 1963 meeting with Chancellor Erhard in Texas. That effort takes many forms. Close consultation with Bonn on East-West negotiations has replaced the unilateral American talks with Moscow that aroused deep suspicions in 1961-62. Reunification of Germany, largely ignored in U. S. statements in 1961-62, is again being highlighted as a Western objective. An increased voice in the West's nuclear strategy is being offered West Germany and other NATO allies through the project for a mixed-manned fleet of twenty-five Polaris ships. In addition, German officers—along with British, French and Italian officers—are to participate in target planning at NATO's Supreme Headquarters near Paris and at the U.S. Strategic Air Command in Omaha. Finally, renewed assurances have been given on the American commitment to Germany's defense, including the use of nuclear weapons, if needed, and the continued presence of six American divisions. The last is the essential foundation for all the rest. For nothing thrusts Germans more rapidly toward a Gaullist view of the world—or toward thoughts of a deal of their own with Russia—than fear of American "disengagement" from Europe.

Taken as a whole, this new policy toward Bonn is aimed neither at a "special relationship" with Germany nor at blocking Franco-German reconciliation. Its objective is to encourage West Germans to seek their future in an integrated European Community that includes France, yet follows a liberal trade policy and maintains close ties with the United States.

The second and more important element in the Ken-

nedy-Johnson strategy comprises a series of concrete programs for joint U.S.-European action on critical problems
within the West and around the world. These projects, designed to link the two North Atlantic continents more
closely as Europe unites, include: (a) the eight-nation multilateral nuclear force, which attempts to meet Europe's desire for a nuclear role while avoiding proliferation of national deterrents to West Germany and other countries; (b)
the plan for Atlantic monetary cooperation now being
elaborated by the ten-nation Paris Group; (c) the proposal
for world agricultural agreements to be negotiated during
the 1964-65 Kennedy Round in Geneva; (d) the Kennedy
Round itself, which will seek substantial tariff reductions
on both shores of the Atlantic; and (e) efforts to find new
ways to help the new nations finance their development.

President Johnson made this strategy his own as soon as
he took office. In his first address to the Congress on November 27, 1963, he dedicated himself to the new "American
dream" of "partnership across the Atlantic." Three weeks
later, in a message to NATO, he pledged "an ever-closer
collaboration between a united Europe and the United
States in dealing with all the great and burdensome tasks of
building and defending a community of free nations." That
pledge, he said, reflected America's awareness "that its security can be assured, its interests and values can be fur-
thered only by a close partnership with Europe in common
tasks . . . [in] defense . . . in monetary affairs, in aid to the
developing areas, and in trade."

These Johnson views were not hastily acquired. Long

before, in numerous speeches as Vice President, he had spelled out his commitment to this objective in greater detail. Many of these speeches were based on drafts prepared in the White House or State Department. But the phrasing showed that Johnson frequently was willing to go beyond established policy to meet some of the most difficult issues head on.

Just twelve days before becoming President, Johnson in Brussels described the multilateral nuclear force (MLF) as only "a first step" toward "a greater European voice in nuclear matters." He went well beyond Kennedy's remarks about a greater future "role and responsibility" for Europe in the MLF. Johnson made it clear that the American veto would become negotiable and he hinted that the MLF could be converted into a European deterrent, if that was what a united Europe later wanted. "Evolution of this missile fleet toward *European control*, as Europe marches toward unity, is by no means excluded," he said.

During the same trip to the Low Countries, Johnson addressed himself to the knottiest economic problem of Atlantic Partnership—agriculture. In a November 7 speech in Amsterdam, he went beyond Kennedy's call for "common agricultural policies across the Atlantic." He indicated agreement with the European view that, to organize the West's agriculture coherently, it would be necessary to coordinate the internal farm programs of the United States and Europe. "If the negotiations involve, as they may, questions of domestic agricultural policy," Johnson said, "we are equally prepared to discuss our domestic policies."

These views reflected a philosophy Johnson had outlined long before, most clearly in a Paris speech on April 16, 1961. That speech foreshadowed Kennedy's Grand Design. It went even further, for it spoke not only of common policies, but of "common institutions" in the Atlantic area. Said Johnson:

> No single nation has enough influence and power to maintain this spacious environment of freedom. The coalition of the peoples and nations of Western Europe and North America is indispensable to this end. . . .
>
> To the United States it is of prime importance to maintain and strengthen the coalition, both for its cohesion and power within the Atlantic area and its capacity for constructive action outside that area. If that cohesion and capacity are to be enhanced, vigorous measures will be required in the political, military and economic fields. . . .
>
> Progress toward an integrated European community will help to enhance that capacity and thus to strengthen the Atlantic Community. . . . The essentially national and loosely coordinated efforts of the past will no longer suffice.
>
> Our end goal . . . should be a true Atlantic Community in which *common institutions will increasingly be developed* to meet common problems. . . .
>
> In progressing toward such a community we can regain the sense of forward movement and imaginative thinking which has characterized the Alliance in its most creative periods.

The challenge that faces Johnson of 1964 is precisely the one defined by the Johnson of 1961. Its essence, as Dean Acheson recently put it, is "to get the Atlantic Community moving again." That can best be done by joint European-American action on concrete programs in the economic and military fields. Such programs will get nowhere through "the essentially national and loosely coordinated" methods employed in the past. New, ad hoc institutions are needed to bring the United States, the Common Market, and Britain together for joint decisions and measures to implement them. Such institutions will achieve nothing if they merely are a cloak for American dominance, or if they lack genuine decision-making power. Europeans will assume the burdens of responsibility only to the degree that the exercise of power is shared. It is this element in American proposals for Atlantic Partnership that will be scrutinized most closely in Europe. This would be so in any circumstances; but it is even more the case at a time when de Gaulle is active in spreading to others his own mistrust of U.S. intentions. Sincere American proposals will need to be explained and defended repeatedly to survive the pinpricks of Gaullist suspicion. Any false currency will be quickly exposed.

If, for example, the project for a multilateral nuclear force is to succeed, Europeans will have to be convinced that the American veto will disappear rather rapidly. It should be made clear, in addition, that the United States, at a later date, will be prepared to "sell its shares," if the Europeans prefer to have an integrated force of their own, coordinated in NATO with American nuclear might. The veto reinforces the Gaullist comment—already widely believed in Europe—that what's involved is "a unilateral American nuclear force, multilaterally financed." The prospect of a European-controlled deterrent, on the other hand, would unite the Governments of the Five and a majority of Frenchmen behind the project; it might even bring the British and

French Governments together in support of the plan, if they were offered, jointly, the leading role. Acceptance by the U.S. Congress should not be impossible, now that such Republican leaders as Nelson Rockefeller and Richard Nixon have publicly advocated a European-controlled deterrent.

If economic expansion is not to be hobbled by monetary instability, the Common Market and Britain must be won to a joint effort with the United States. Atlantic monetary cooperation is essential not only to protect the dollar and to head off the world "liquidity" problem of the future, but to lay a sound basis for intensified Atlantic cooperation across the whole spectrum of economic problems facing the West. The chief reform needed is one that gives the moneys of the Common Market countries a major reserve-currency role, thus lightening the load on the dollar. Achieving this will require some sacrifice of American monetary dominance and an increased voice for Europe in managing the currency of the West.

If development of the new nations is to be financed adequately, Europe's cooperation must be enlisted for a new approach. Grants and loans are pushing up against budget ceilings in all the donor countries. The need now is for trade to supplement aid by helping the world's poor nations finance their own industrialization out of increased export earnings. The Common Market is the world's biggest importer. Its cooperation is essential if, for example, world commodity prices are to be stabilized at a level that provides the raw-materials-exporting countries with a fair return on their labor. Only the U.S. and Europe, working together as the world's chief importers and raw-materials consumers, can accomplish this. The Common Market countries, including France, have expressed support for the idea, just as did the Kennedy Administration. The time has come for President Johnson to fit these words to action. Successful action will require moving in the direction of joint U.S.-European boards with limited but real powers to work out price, output and trade arrangements with the producing countries. Only in this way can we avoid a class war between rich and poor nations that, in this century, could prove just as disastrous as was the failure of Europe's Governments in the last century to come to grips in time with their own domestic class conflicts.

If the "Kennedy Round" of tariff and trade liberalization is to be successful in the agricultural field, it must go far beyond the policies epitomized by Secretary Freeman's "chicken war" and his futile drive to maintain U.S. farm exports to Europe at past levels. The U.S. effort in Geneva in 1964 will have to focus on the attempt that will be made, starting with grain, to solve the surplus problem through world agreements—a proposal that France originated and still supports. Effective agreements would require readiness by the U.S. and other countries to accept some degree of international control over farm prices, subsidies, production management, exports, and surplus disposal. If the main importing and exporting countries—the U.S., the Common Market, Britain and the Commonwealth—can create joint decision-making machinery for these purposes, Atlantic partnership would begin to mean something. And the piling up of surplus stocks, while most of the world goes hungry, could be ended.

Joint enterprises of this kind can create a durable U.S.-European partnership only if power, sovereignty, and burdens are shared. And, in fact, there is no real alternative. Whatever may be thought by some of the Goldwater faction in America and some of the Gaullist faction in Europe, neither continent any longer can "go it alone" in the world.

The Cold War can be eased by persistent negotiation, as the test ban accord has shown. But the challenge of the East —whether primarily Russian, Chinese or Sino-Soviet—is sure to continue. That challenge hinges on faith in the inevitability of a Communist world and determination to bring that Communist world about. There will be no stable peace until that faith and that determination are shaken. They can be shaken only by Western unity. It must be demonstrated that the non-Communist world can solve its political, military, economic, and social problems, that the United States and a uniting Europe are moving to construct a society that is as dynamic as it is viable.

Neither the United States nor Europe can solve the West's critical problems alone. The Common Market, despite its current difficulties, makes it possible for the U.S. and a revived Europe, which ultimately must include Britain, to undertake a joint approach. The uniting of Europe thus continues to be in the American interest even if it involves, as it must, some discrimination against American trade. The United States must remain in the future, as in the past, the catalyst in bringing Europe's unity about. At the same time, common U.S.-European programs must be shaped and given institutional form without awaiting the entry of Britain into the Common Market. If an Atlantic Partnership gradually is to be constructed, Washington must take the initiative. In doing so, it will have to face the fact that partnership, by definition, can be achieved only if power is shared.

It is no longer possible to preach supranational principles to Europe and to practice national decision-making in the United States. The day is past when Washington can urge European nations to integrate, yet insist on complete freedom of action for itself. A "ferment of change" has been introduced into the world by the resurgence of Europe and the new method devised there to unite nations for common action. It may be a long time before Americans are prepared to go as far as Europeans in sharing sovereignty, but the first steps must now be taken on a problem-by-problem basis to adapt the European method to the Atlantic basin.

In nuclear matters, monetary affairs, agriculture, aid to the developing nations and in other fields, American initiatives can spur the concept of joint U.S.-European efforts. But the key to success lies in a progressive sharing of decision-making power along with the financial burdens of free-world responsibility.

As Europeans are won to such proposals, de Gaulle either will go along or face isolation, something he dislikes intensely. In either case, the way will have been prepared for the Atlantic Partnership that must follow—and could very well precede—de Gaulle's departure from the public scene.

Chronology

1950

MAY The Schuman Plan, inspired by Jean Monnet, proposes that France and West Germany pool their coal and steel under a supranational authority open to other European countries as a first step toward European federal union. Six nations—France, West Germany, Italy, Belgium, Netherlands, Luxembourg—accept; Britain refuses.

OCTOBER European Defense Community proposed, and same six countries agree to draft a treaty; Britain refuses.

1952

MAY European Defense Community Treaty signed.

JULY Schuman Plan treaty ratified establishing European Coal and Steel Community; Jean Monnet appointed President of the High Authority.

1954

AUGUST European Defense Community defeated in French Assembly.

1955

JUNE Six-nation Messina Conference appoints Spaak Committee to study integration in economic, atomic fields; Britain is observer, then withdraws.

OCTOBER Monnet launches Action Committee for the United States of Europe with top leaders of all major non-Communist unions and political parties of the Six countries (except the Gaullists in France).

1956

JUNE Spaak Committee begins drafting Euratom and Common Market Treaties.

JULY Britain proposes seventeen-nation Free Trade Area and Nuclear Energy Agency.

1957

MARCH Common Market and Euratom Treaties signed in Rome.

1958

JANUARY Common Market and Euratom Treaties go into effect.

MAY Officers and settlers revolt in Algiers.

JUNE De Gaulle returns to power.

SEPTEMBER De Gaulle writes Eisenhower and Macmillan proposing reorganization of NATO and a triumvirate of U.S., Britain, and France to shape West's global strategy.

NOVEMBER Khrushchev's "ultimatum" opens prolonged Berlin crisis.

NOVEMBER Seventeen-nation Free Trade Area negotiations collapse.

1959

JANUARY Common Market begins to function with first tariff cuts among the Six.

FEBRUARY Britain launches plan for seven-nation European Free Trade Association (EFTA).

MARCH His proposal for tripartite directorate evaded by Eisenhower and Macmillan, de Gaulle withdraws French

Mediterranean Fleet from NATO, continues refusal to accept IRBMs and U.S. atomic stockpiles on French soil.

JUNE U.S. announces progressive withdrawal of fighter-bombers from France for lack of atomic stockpiles.

JUNE Monnet proposes "partnership" between the U.S. and Europe; proposal, taken up by Douglas Dillon, leads to creation of twenty-nation Organization for Economic Cooperation and Development (OECD) with U.S. and Canada as members.

SEPTEMBER Eisenhower flies to Paris to consult de Gaulle before Khrushchev visit to United States.

SEPTEMBER Eisenhower-Khrushchev meeting at Camp David.

NOVEMBER EFTA Convention signed by the "Outer Seven"—Britain, Norway, Sweden, Denmark, Austria, Switzerland, Portugal.

DECEMBER Eisenhower meets with de Gaulle and Macmillan in Paris to plan Summit conference with Khrushchev.

1960

FEBRUARY First French atomic explosion in Sahara.

MARCH Khrushchev visit to France.

APRIL Second French atomic explosion.

APRIL De Gaulle-Macmillan meeting at Buckingham Palace.

APRIL De Gaulle visit to United States.

MAY The Six take first "acceleration" decision to speed up tariff reductions and hasten full Common Market.

MAY Four-Power East-West Summit in Paris aborts in wake of U-2 incident.

AUGUST De Gaulle broaches plan for European Confederation in Rambouillet meeting with Adenauer; West German Chancellor approves plan, but changes mind few days later.

AUGUST Macmillan visits Bonn, sounds out Adenauer on possible British move to enter the new Europe.

SEPTEMBER De Gaulle discusses Confederation plan with Premiers of Italy, Belgium, Holland, Luxembourg, and makes outline public at press conference.

OCTOBER French Premier Debre in Bonn seeks to soothe Adenauer's doubts.

NOVEMBER Monnet urges influential Action Committee to accept amended version of de Gaulle's Confederation plan as a first step toward federal union.

DECEMBER Adenauer meets de Gaulle in Paris, agrees to Summit meeting of the Six to advance Confederation plan.

1961

JANUARY Macmillan sees de Gaulle at Rambouillet, indicates interest in joining or associating with Common Market.

FEBRUARY Summit meeting of the Six in Paris; Fouchet committee to be appointed to study Confederation plan.

FEBRUARY French, British experts meet, explore British membership in or association with EEC.

MARCH French Foreign Minister Couve de Murville publicly urges "a change of mind" by London and British entry into the Common Market.

MARCH Heath asks George Ball how U.S. would react to a British decision to join Common Market.

APRIL Kennedy-Macmillan meeting in Washington.

JUNE Kennedy-de Gaulle meeting in Paris goes well.

JUNE De Gaulle declares Britain should enter Common Market.

JULY Summit meeting of the Six in Bonn agrees to draft treaty for political union.

JULY 31 Macmillan announces Britain's decision to apply for membership in Common Market.

AUGUST De Gaulle rejects Rusk-Kennedy proposal for Foreign Ministers' conference with Russia on Berlin.

AUGUST 13 Berlin Wall erected.

SEPTEMBER De Gaulle publicly welcomes British application for Common Market.

OCTOBER 10 Heath opens British-Common Market negotiations.

NOVEMBER Macmillan-de Gaulle meeting at Birch Grove.

DECEMBER First "split" communique in NATO history; NATO Council votes 14 to 1, against France, to continue contacts with Russia on Berlin.

Chronology

1962

JANUARY De Gaulle repudiates French concessions in Fouchet Committee on political union treaty.

JANUARY 14 Six reach agreement on common agricultural policy and Common Market enters Second Stage.

FEBRUARY De Gaulle visits Adenauer in Baden-Baden, yields to main German conditions on political union of Six.

MARCH Algerian War ends with Evian cease-fire agreement.

APRIL 4 De Gaulle flies to Turin, appeases Fanfani on political union.

APRIL 10 Heath bids for British entry into political union talks.

APRIL 17 Breakdown of negotiations on European political union; Dutch, supported by Belgians, refuse to form political union without Britain.

APRIL 18 Kennedy reaffirms policy of no nuclear aid to France after major reappraisal that splits cabinet.

MAY 4-6 NATO Ministerial Conference at Athens; "McNamara Doctrine" urges defense of Europe with conventional forces primarily; Britain continues support for U.S. talks with Russia, which are opposed by French, Germans.

MAY 12 After seven months of sparring, real negotiations begin between Britain and Common Market in Brussels.

JUNE 2-3 De Gaulle-Macmillan meetings at Chateau des Champs.

JUNE 16 McNamara speech at Ann Arbor expounds theory of "controlled response" and criticizes small national deterrents.

JULY 4 Kennedy in Philadelphia speech endorses Atlantic Partnership.

AUGUST 1-5 Brussels negotiations fail to agree on Commonwealth issues before summer recess.

SEPTEMBER 2-9 De Gaulle's tour of Germany; he proposes Franco-German Treaty.

SEPTEMBER 12-19 Conference of Commonwealth Prime Ministers, London.

OCTOBER 2-4 Labor Party Conference.

OCTOBER 10-13 Conservative Party Conference.

OCTOBER 22 Kennedy speech on Cuban missile crisis.

OCTOBER 25-27 Brussels negotiations bog down over issue of British domestic agriculture.

NOVEMBER 9 McNamara phones British Defense Minister Thorneycroft that U.S. is considering abandonment of Skybolt program.

NOVEMBER 25 De Gaulle emerges victorious from French national elections.

DECEMBER 11 Thorneycroft meets with McNamara in London to discuss Skybolt crisis.

DECEMBER 13-15 NATO Ministerial conference in Paris; McNamara says there is no military requirement for a NATO nuclear force.

DECEMBER 15-16 De Gaulle and Macmillan meet at Rambouillet.

DECEMBER 18-21 Kennedy-Macmillan at Nassau; agreement on Polaris and multilateral NATO nuclear force.

1963

JANUARY 14 De Gaulle at press conference bars Britain from Common Market and rejects Polaris offer.

JANUARY 23 Adenauer meets de Gaulle in Paris, signs Franco-German Treaty.

JANUARY 29 Couve de Murville halts Brussels negotiations.

MAY West German Bundestag ratifies Franco-German Treaty with preamble insisting on federal union of Europe, NATO reinforcement, and close U.S. ties.

JUNE Kennedy tour of Europe restores close relationship with Germany; Paulskirche speech in Frankfurt outlines new strategy for Atlantic Partnership.

JULY Acceleration of Common Market tariff cuts, agreed in Spring, goes into effect, also new agreement on aid to former African territories, mostly French.

JULY First Adenauer-de Gaulle conference in Bonn under Franco-German treaty goes badly. A few days later, de Gaulle yields to German insistence on "contacts" with Britain. Germans, in return, give ground on agricultural issues of interest to France.

JULY 29 De Gaulle warns Common Market must be extended to agriculture by end of year or "disappear."

AUGUST Kennedy recognizes France as nuclear power eligible for U.S. aid without new legislation . . . if it co-operates on NATO and other defense issues.

OCTOBER Adenauer's retirement; Erhard becomes Chancellor, promising policy closer to that of U.S. and Britain. Macmillan replaced as Prime Minister by Sir Alec Douglas-Home, who favors multilateral nuclear force. Couve de Murville announces that de Gaulle will visit Kennedy in 1964, probably early in year. Negotiations begin in Paris looking toward drafting eight-nation treaty for the NATO nuclear force; Britain participates, France refuses.

NOVEMBER 22 Kennedy assassinated; Johnson becomes President.

NOVEMBER 25 Johnson and de Gaulle agree to meet in 1964 for "thorough examination" of Franco-American differences, but few days later disagree over site of meeting.

NOVEMBER 27 Johnson, continuing Kennedy policy, commits himself to support European union and "new American dream" of "Atlantic Partnership."

DECEMBER 23 Agreement at Brussels extends Common Market to most of agriculture in Franco-German compromise.

DECEMBER 28-29 Johnson and Erhard in Texas agree on negotiating with Russia and strengthening Atlantic community.

DECEMBER 31 De Gaulle in year-end speech favors new moves in 1964 toward political union as urged by Erhard, including merger of executive commissions of the three European economic communities.

1964

JANUARY 27 De Gaulle announces recognition of Communist China.